"Anyone seriously interested in systems thinking should read this book. Morin takes us on a telescopic journey through space and time, tracing the dynamics of a complex evolution toward a planetary culture. A breathtaking achievement in social thought!"
　　—Ronald E. Purser, San Francisco State University

"*Homeland Earth* is a powerful and brilliantly written vision that can guide human, social, and global evolution. Based on a solid understanding of evolutionary principles, the authors convincingly explain the solution of the seemingly antagonistic goals of preserving our cultural and natural diversities and at the same time engaging in a transformative revolutionary change by which humanity can realize itself as 'one and whole,' as a global community of nations."
　　—Bela H. Banathy, Saybrook Graduate School
　　and International Systems Institute

"This book illustrates Edgar Morin's unique talent for articulating unsettling paradoxes. He alerts us to the dangers inherent in our imprudent refusal to acknowledge our limits when confronted with complex problems. Prudence, however, forms only one half of Morin's message for he also urges us to take risks by assuming the fraternal responsibilities of the planetary citizens we are fast becoming. But to do so, reason must first be rescued from technical rationality."
　　—Laurent Dobuzinskis, Simon Fraser University

"A deeply intelligent exploration of our place in this Earth, and of the evolutionary moment and potential at which we stand."
　　—Allan Combs, University of North Carolina and
　　author of *The Radiance of Being: Complexity, Chaos,
　　and the Evolution of Consciousness*

Homeland Earth

A Manifesto for the New Millennium

ADVANCES IN SYSTEMS THEORY, COMPLEXITY, AND THE HUMAN SCIENCES

Alfonso Montuori, Series Editor

Homeland Earth

A Manifesto for the New Millennium

Edgar Morin
Anne Brigitte Kern

translated by Sean M. Kelly and Roger LaPointe

HAMPTON PRESS, INC.
CRESSKILL, NEW JERSEY

Printed in the United State of America

Library of Congress Cataloging-in-Publication Data

Morin, Edgar.
    [Terre-patrie. English]
    Homeland earth : a manifesto for the new millenium / Edgar Morin, Anne Brigitte Kern
        p. cm. -- (Advances in systems theory, complexity, and the human sciences)
    Includes bibliographical references
    ISBN 1-57273-248-2
    1. Environmental policy. 2. Social ecology. 3. Civilization.
I. Kern, Anne Brigitte. II. Title. III. Series
GE170.M6713 1998
304.2--dc21   98-35125
                                       CIP

Hampton Press, Inc.
23 Broadway
Cresskill, NJ 07626

Contents

Series Editor's Foreword

Edgar Morin has written that, in a world with an ever-increasing creation and transmission of new data, new information, and new events, one of the main problems facing humanity today is the way in which we organize knowledge. In this book, Morin addresses this problem using what he calls "complex thought." He helps us think about our Homeland Earth, about where we have come from, who we are, and where we might go.

Morin first of all *contextualizes* our homeland, in time and space. He shows us the larger planetary context we live in, its history both cosmic and cultural. But he also constantly links the global and the singular, macro and micro, part and whole, figure and ground. He reminds us that all knowledge involves a knower, and that this knower is engaged in a constant, complex process by which knowledge is created, critiqued, connected, discussed, and then perhaps rejected. Knowledge emerges and lives in a broader planetary ecology of physiosphere, biosphere, and noosphere. And knowledge is biodegradable, writes Morin, just as human knowers are.

Morin's "complex thought," developed during a remarkable career begun just after World War II, and developed most extensively in the four volumes of "La Methode," arises out of a critique of fragmented, decontextualized, abstract, and disjunctive thinking. While drawing on systems theory, cybernetics, and information theory, Morin goes beyond them to tackle fundamental problems of human co-existence in an attempt to link all of the sciences. But his effort is not to create a great, all-encompassing synthesis, but rather a polyphonic, "unitas multiplex," a continuous "en-cyclo-pedic" journey through the various domains of human knowledge in a multidimensional effort to bring together what was torn asunder, all the time remaining vividly aware of the dangers that lie in "total" knowledge and the potentials that lie in our ignorance, our uncertainty, and our ambivalence.

For Morin, one of the vital aspects of complex thought is the acknowledgment of disorder, or uncertainty and ambiguity. Indeed, our planetary journey is fraught with uncertainty, and for Morin this recognition is both tragic and a source of hope. Whereas most conceptual frameworks have historically attempted to order the world in a closed, "totalizing" manner, Morin insists that any attempt to eliminate, homogenize, or ignore uncertainty and disorder is mutilating and self-deceptive. Morin accepts fully the openness of our journey, the potential for both chaos and creativity, confusion and complexity—and the importance at all times of our decisions and choices.

Disorder and uncertainty become, in Morin's "complex thought," not simply errors to be avoided or simplified or rationalized, but opportunities for learning and change. Morin recognizes the generative and creative dimensions of diversity, and therefore urges us to approach this diversity in ways that celebrate polyphone and engage fully the richness of our world without seeking security in ready-made belief systems that deny the complexity of our experience.

With the collapse of commonly agreed-on notions of progress, we are faced with a "crisis of the future." The relationship between past, present, and future is not a determined, linear progression. The future is uncertain. "Salvation," whether economic, social, psychological, or spiritual, is not at hand. The future cannot be predicted, and the principle of the "ecology of action" shows that even the most well-intentioned initiatives, once set in motion, escape our control and may indeed have effects diametrically opposed to our intentions. How are we to live in such a world, with a seemingly endless plurality of perspectives, ideologies, methodologies, and interests? How are we to live in a world where uncertainty, ambiguity, and disorder will never be completely eliminated, but lie at the very heart of our knowledge? Where knowledge cannot be pure, purified, pristine, and free of the presence of context and of the knower? These are the vital questions that Morin masterfully addresses in these pages.

Morin does not present us with utopian futures, determined by inevitable technological, political, or spiritual progress, nor with dystopian futures, negative mirror images of those same forces. His are not easy technological "solutions" nor facile calls for "global unity." There is not attempt to scare us with gloomy scenarios or the glib predictions of popular futurism. Morin does recognize the endless tragedies that have plagued our history, both local and global, and that play themselves out every day, while at the same time acknowledging those elements of human solidarity that give us cause for hope, but more than that, are a call to reflection and action. His work is an invitation to think deeply about our situation, and to think about our world and ourselves differently. It is an invitation to think and act creatively and to participate in the journey of Homeland Earth with both wisdom and compassion.

Alfonso Montuori
Series Editor

Preface

Homeland Earth is a passionate and compelling summation of Morin's synthetic vision of our planetary history and collective destiny. As we approach the end of the millennium, there is much talk of a "new world order" and a "new paradigm" struggling to emerge. At the same time, however, there is a sense of increasing disorder, chaos, and crisis on a global scale. Never before has there been a greater need for a truly planetary perspective—a perspective at once political, ecological, philosophical, and ethical—on the vital crises with which humanity is currently faced. In refreshing contrast to the tedious obscurity and precious irrelevance of most academic writing, and avoiding the journalistic superficiality of the popularizers, *Homeland Earth* provides such a perspective, and one, moreover, which is accessible to a correspondingly wide spectrum of readers.

As this book will most likely constitute Morin's introduction to the English speaking world, I thought it would be appropriate to preface it with a few words about the man and his ideas.[1] Edgar Morin was born in Paris in 1921 to a non-practicing Jewish family of

---

[1] I know of only one book-length treatment of Morin's life and ideas—J.B. Fages' *Comprendre Edgar Morin* [Understanding Edgar Morin] (Toulouse: Privat, 1980). Morin himself has published several personalized accounts of

the Mediterranean "Diaspora." An otherwise happy childhood was marked by the tragic death of his mother when Edgar was barely ten. His solitary adolescence, during which he immersed himself in the imaginal worlds of European literature, gradually gave way to intense engagement in political discussions while pursuing studies in history, philosophy, economics, and law at the Sorbonne. During the Nazi occupation, Morin joined the French Resistance and multiplied his contacts and activities among various circles of left-wing intellectuals. A turning-point came in 1951 when he was effectively ex-communicated from the Communist party for his increasingly critical attitude to the Stalinist regime. The same year, however, saw the publication of his first major synthetic work—*L'Homme et la mort* [The Human Meaning of Death] (Le Seuil, 1951)—a masterpiece of dialectical thinking and of interdisciplinary reflection on the pivotal role of death in the history of our species.

For nearly the next two decades, up to and including his involvement as "participant-observer" in the student revolution of May '68, Morin took on greater responsibilities as director of research at the Centre national de la recherche scientifique and devoted himself, for the most part, to analyzing the mythopoeic dimensions of popular culture, on the one hand,[2] and to developing a new "sociology of the present," on the other.[3]

---

his work in progress at various critical points in the history of his intellectual development—beginning with *Autocritique* (Le Seuil, 1959), followed by *Le Vif du sujet* [untranslatable: perhaps, The Living Subject] (Le Seuil, 1969), *Le Journal de Californie* [The California Journal] (Le Seuil, 1970), *Journal d'un livre* [A Book Journal] (Inter-Editions, 1981), and finally his retrospective intellectual autobiography, *Mes Demons* [My Daimones] (Stock, 1994). The most in-depth treatment of Morin in English is Myron Kofman's *From Big Brother to Fraternity* (London and Chicago: Pluto Press, 1996), which includes a detailed treatment of Morin's major work, *La Methode*. See also my two articles: "Hegel and Morin: The Science of Wisdom and the Wisdom of the New Science," in *The Owl of Minerva: Biannual Journal of the Hegel Society of America, 20*(1), 51-67, 1988; and "Beyond Materialism and Idealism: Reflections on the Work of David Bohm and Edgar Morin," in *Idealistic Studies, xxxii*(1), 28-38, 1992.

[2]*Le Cinema ou l'homme imaginaire* [The Cinema, or Imaginal Man] (Minuit, 1956), Les Stars [Stars] (Le Seuil, 1957), *L'Espirit du temps* [Spirit of the Age] (Grasset, 1962).

[3]*Commune en France* [A commune in France] (Fayard, 1967), *Mai 68* [May, 1968] (Fayard, 1968), *La Rumeur d'Orleans* [The Rumour of Orleans] (Le Seuil, 1969). See also his collection of essays, *Sociologie* [Sociology] (Fayard, 1984/1994).

Another turning-point came in 1969-70 when Morin accepted an invitation from the *Salk Institute for Biological Research* in California. Here he was profoundly influenced by the communal and ecological sensibility of the Counter-Culture, as well as by ongoing discussions about cybernetics, Systems Theory, and new developments in the life sciences. The first fruit of this encounter was his book, *Le paradigme perdu* [Paradigm Lost] (Le Seuil, 1973), in which Morin sought to revision the question of human origins. It was here that he first clearly articulated the necessity for a *Scienza nuova*—a "fundamental anthropology"—which respects the irreducible complexity of the human phenomenon and conceives of human evolution in terms of a dialectic among such normally mutually exclusive terms as nature and culture, the individual, the species, and society—terms which together constitute "one single bio-psycho-socio-cultural system." (Morin 1973, 146) It was here, too, that he first proposed his view of human nature as *homo sapiens/demens,* which recognizes that what distinguishes human beings from other animals is not merely the ability to reason and make tools, but also the ability to imagine and feel with unparalleled intensity. "The genius of sapiens," writes Morin, "lies in the intercommunication between the imaginary and the real, the logical and the affective, the speculative and the existential, the unconscious and the conscious, subject and object. . . ." (ibid., 144)

The culmination of this phase of Morin's development, however, has been the production of his most ambitious work, *La Methode* [Method] (Le Seuil), four volumes of which have so far appeared (I: *La Nature de la Nature* [The Nature of Nature] [1977], II: *La Vie de la Vie* The Life of Life] [1980], III: *La Connaissance de la Connaissance* [The Knowing of Knowing] [1986], and IV: *Les Idees* [Ideas] [1991]). The method in question is the "way" (*meta + hodos*=way) of the new science—which is now conceived not only as "fundamental anthropology," but as the "science of science"—a way which can lead us to "re-member the mutilated, articulate the disjointed, and think the obscured." (1977, 23) In contrast with modern or classical science, which is governed—for the most part unconsciously—by the paradigm of simplification or disjunction, the new science is consciously informed by the paradigm of *complexity* (*com-plexere*= to weave together, to encompass). This paradigm, however, does not stand in absolute opposition to that of disjunction.(for this would amount to another disjunction), but rather includes the latter as one moment of "an active and generative process." (ibid., 382)

Morin draws particular attention to three related principles of complexity. The first is the principle of dialogic, which Morin now distinguishes from his earlier use of the Hegelian dialectic by stressing the persistence of dynamic tension between the terms in question. The dialogic, as Morin puts it, is "the symbiotic combination of . . . two logics, a combination...that is at once complementary, concurrent, and antagonistic." (*Science avec conscience*, [Science with Consciousness/conscience], Fayard, 1982, 287) The second is the principle of recursivity, which flows from the dialogic, and back to it again, in the manner of a loop or circle. A process is recursive, writes Morin, when it "produces the elements or effects necessary for its own generation or existence, a circuitous process whereby the product or ultimate effect becomes a prime element and first cause." (Morin, 1977, 186) The third is the holographic principle, which can be understood as the recursive dialogic of part and whole. This principle recognizes that "the whole is in a certain manner included...in the part which is included in the whole." (Morin, 1986, 102)

Throughout *La Methode*, Morin demonstrates the fruitfulness—and indeed the indispensability—of these principles for understanding the complex character of any system, or organization (to use Morin's preferred term)—whether physical, biological, or anthropo-social. All organizations—from atoms to galaxies, from cells to societies—are seen to involve a recursive dialogic between order and disorder (terms which subsume such analogous pairs as necessity and chance, constraints and possibilities, information and noise, etc.) as well as between the organization and its environment or eco-system.

The central insight and great refrain of *La Methode*, however, is that the revolution which has occurred (and is still occurring) in our knowledge of organization calls for a corresponding revolution in the organization of knowledge. This is especially true of our understanding of the relation between the natural and the human sciences which, under the influence of the paradigm of disjunction, have tended to develop in parallel isolation. For if it is true that all human or anthropo-social knowledge is in some sense the product of, and dependent upon, the physical and biological processes studied by the natural sciences, it is equally true that the models and theories which describe and define these processes are themselves the product of individual scientists and the larger anthropo-social context in which they are embedded.[4] The complex (i.e., dialogical, recursive, and holographic) truth that "physical knowledge depends upon anthropo-social knowledge which depends upon physical knowledge" (Morin, 1977, 12) can be represented as follows:

---

[4]For instance, just as the thermodynamical notions of energy and entropy bear the stamp of the Industrial Revolution during which they were forged, so the notions of information and programs, notions which have become so vital to biological thinking, are analogs transferred from the contemporary world of computers and telecommunications.

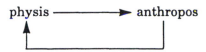

Within the paradigm of disjunction, this kind of relation would be branded as a logical absurdity or vicious circle. For the new paradigm, by contrast, this relation points to "the possibility of transforming vicious circles into virtuous cycles which, in the process, become reflexive and generative of complex thinking." (ibid., 19)

Nowhere is the need for such complex thinking more apparent than when trying to elucidate the contemporary global predicament. Morin's 1981 book, *Pour sortir du XXe siecle* [Surviving the 20th Century] (Nathan, 1981), was already looking forward to the year 2,000 as a kind of symbolic attractor of the process of globalization wherein "crisis, progression, regression, and revolution mingle and are transmuted . . . into one another" (back cover). This was followed in 1983 by his book, *De la nature de l'U.R.S.S.* [On the Nature of the Soviet Union] (Fayard)—a prescient analysis of Soviet totalitarianism[5]—and by *Penser l'Europe* [The Idea of Europe] (Gallimard, 1987), a book which explores the complex factors, both historical and current, involved in the idea of a unified European community. Following the collapse of the Soviet empire, Morin (in collaboration with Mauro Ceruti and Gianluca Bocchi) published *Un nouveau commencement* [A new Beginning] (Le Seuil, 1991)—a collection of essays which focus on the 20th century, up to and including the Soviet collapse, as the "Damoclean phase" of the "Planetary Iron Age."

Homeland Earth (*Terre-Patrie*, Le Seuil, 1993) is the capstone of the series that began with *Pour sortir du XXe siecle*. Apart from the sense of urgency with which it is pervaded, what most distinguishes it from its predecessors is the manner in which it sustains a truly planetary perspective on the complex factors (ecological, technological, social, psychological) which might facilitate, as they threaten to abort, a nascent humanity. "The symptoms of death and birth," as the authors indicated on the back cover to the French edition, "merge into one another. This situation is not merely the result of various kinds of crisis superadded to traditional conflicts, . . . it is a whole which feeds upon these conflictual, crisis-ridden, and problematical ingredients and which

---

[5]Prescient because Morin clearly foresaw, as a function of the paradoxical combination of infinite strength with infinite weakness, that the Soviet Empire, following a rupture at the top, could easily see a period of reform leading to disintegration.

encompasses, overruns, and feeds them in return. And this whole contains the problem of problems: the inability of humanity to become humanity."

Chapter One of *Homeland Earth* outlines the history of the Planetary Era, from its birth around 1,500 C.E. with the voyages of discovery, through the period of colonial domination and techno-industrial expansion, to the contemporary emergence, following the World Wars, of a new world order/disorder and the lineaments of a first planetary consciousness.

Chapter Two, "Citizens of the Earth," illustrates the cosmological, ecological, and anthropological solidarity of this planetary consciousness through a concise synthesis of the revolutionary breakthroughs in astrophysics, the Earth sciences, biology, paleontology, and anthropology from the latter part of this century.

Chapter Three, "The Earth in Crisis," returns to the new world order/disorder to consider the various interlocking and mutually reinforcing crises—economic, demographic, political, and ecological—which currently beset the Planet.

Chapter Four, "Our Terrestrial Goals," sets forth the principles of a global ethics and discusses the complex relation between such imperatives as the need for unification and diversification, resistance, preservation, and change in the pursuit of ongoing hominization.

Chapter Five, "Impossible Realism," stresses the radical uncertainty of historical processes, particularly in this fifth century of the Planetary Era, steering a middle course between a potentially despairing realism, on the one hand, and utopian idealism, on the other.

Chapter Six, "Anthropolitics," calls for a humanizing of the political arena through the recognition of its necessary insertion in the social, biological, planetary, and indeed cosmic dimensions of our human nature.

Chapter Seven, "The Reform in Thinking," makes explicit the key principles of the paradigm of complexity—focusing on the dialogical and recursive relation between part and whole (or the local and the global)—that has informed the argument of the preceding chapters.

The final chapter, "The Gospel of Doom," is a passionate plea for the renouncement of hope in any final salvation—whether other-worldly or of this world—and the embracement of our common destiny as citizens of this, our Homeland Earth.

Sean M. Kelly, Ottawa, 1998

Prologue:
The History of History

PREHISTORY AND HISTORY

For tens of thousands of years, "archaic" societies of hunter gatherers spread across the Earth. They became strangers to one another through distance, language, rites, beliefs, and mores. They became differentiated, some of them open and liberal, others closed and constraining, some with diffuse or collective authority, others with concentrated authority. However diverse they became, they constituted a first fundamental type of society for *homo sapiens* (Morin, 1979). For several tens of millennia, this diaspora of archaic societies, each one ignoring the other, constituted humanity.

The development of urban/rural civilizations ignored, then destroyed, this humanity. The spread of historical societies banished the archaic to the forests and deserts, where they were discovered and soon annihilated by the explorers and prospectors of the Planetary Era. At present, with but rare exceptions, they are definitively assassinated, without their assassins having assimilated the most important part of their age-old wisdom. History, pitiless toward the vanquished historical civilizations, has been relentlessly atrocious toward everything prehistoric. Prehistory did not fade

1

away—it was exterminated. The founders of the cultures and societies of *homo sapiens* are the victims of a systematic genocide on the part of humanity, which has, in this way, made progress in parricide.

Perhaps 10,000 years ago, history was born in Mesopotamia, 4,000 years ago in Egypt, 2,500 years ago in the Indus valley and in the Huang Po valley. Through a tremendous sociological metamorphosis, small societies without agriculture, government, towns, and armies, gave way to cities, kingdoms, and empires, with populations in the tens of thousands, then hundreds of thousands, even millions, that also included agriculture, cities, government, division of labor, social classes, war, slavery, and great religions and civilizations.

This history is the rise, growth, multiplication, and fight to the death of states among themselves. It is conquest, invasion, subjugation, and it is resistance, revolt, and insurrection. It is battles, ruins, coups, and conspiracies, and it is the spread of power and force, the excessiveness of power. It is the terrifying reign of gods that thirst for blood. It is mass subjugation and mass murder. It is the erection of palaces, temples, and grandiose pyramids. It is the development of technology and the arts, and it is the invention and development of writing.[1] It is the trading of goods and ideas by land and sea. It is also, here and there, a message of pity and compassion, here and there a questioning of the mystery of the world.

History is sound and fury, but at the same time it is the constitution of great civilizations that believe themselves to be eternal, even though most would pass away. So it was with pharaonic Egypt, Assyria, Babylonia, the Minoan empire, the Dravidians, the Etruscans, the Olmecs, Athens, the Persians, Rome, the Mayans, the Toltecs, the Zapotecs, Byzantium, Angkor, the Aztecs, the Incas, the Sassanids, the Ottomans, the Habsburgs, the Third Reich, and the U.S.S.R. Whereas the Roman empire only lasted a few centuries, the only ones to last for millennia, despite invasions and the toppling of dynasties, were the two stable seats of civilization in India and, especially, China.

Traditional history has told us the story of the sound and fury of battles, coups, and insane ambitions. It has ridden wave-crests and whirlwinds, in which the so-called "new history" saw only the foam of contingency. This new history, now considerably aged,

---

[1]Around 3000 B.C.: hieroglyphics in Egypt, pictograms in Mesopotamia. Around 1500-1400 B.C.: ideographs in China; linear B in Crete and Greece; Hittite cuneiform in Anatolia. Around 1100 B.C.: the Phoenicians invented the alphabet.

thought it had uncovered the truth of becoming in the form of socioeconomic determinism. It then started to become more polydimensional and ethnographically sensitive. Today, contingency, which has made its appearance in the physical and biological sciences, is being reintroduced to the historical sciences. It is no longer seen as mere foam, but as the falls, rapids, and changes of course in the torrent of history.

Despite a growing openness to the contingent, the socioeconomic, the ethnographic, and sometimes even the polydimensional, the history of historians must also become anthropological. Historical anthropology would have to consider the orders, disorders, and organization that oppose one another and combine and intermix throughout historical periods in correlation with the forces of order-disorder-organization proper to the mind/brain of *homo sapiens demens*. It would have to consider the diverse forms of social organization that have appeared in historical times, from pharaonic Egypt and Periclean Athens to contemporary democracies and totalitarianisms, as so many emergences of anthroposocial potentials. It would have to consider the wars, massacres, slavery, murder, torture, fanaticisms, along with faith, its sublime transports, and philosophy, as actualizations of anthropological potentials. It would consider such individuals as Akhenaton, Alexander, Napoleon, Stalin, Hitler, and de Gaulle as concretizations and actualizations of the potentials of *homo sapiens demens*.

We need a multidimensional and anthropological history, which would include its ingredients of sound and fury, of disorder and death. The history of historians lags behind, anthropologically speaking, the tragedies of the Greeks, the Elizabethans, and particularly Shakespeare, which have shown that the tragedies of history were the tragedies of human passion, excess, and blindness.

Grandeur and horror, sublimities and atrocities, splendor and misery, the ambivalent and complex realities of "human nature" (e.g., see Morin, 1979) find fabulous expression in history, whose adventure continues to unfold and exasperate itself in our own current Planetary Era. Today, the destiny of humanity raises with extreme insistence the key question: Can we find our way out of this history? Is this adventure the only path before us?

THE GREAT HISTORIES

Beginning with what we call Antiquity, and continuing for 5,000 years, history has unfolded across the various continents. However, by the 14th century, it still had not become planetary. There had been, instead, many Histories, with very little communication among them. Nevertheless, the great civilizations, with their military or navigational expansion, began to discover the Earth. There were tremendous drives, grandiose yet ephemeral, to conquer the world, headed by names such as Genghis Khan, Tamberlain. There were grand maritime adventures toward the unknown at the ends of the world, as with the Vikings who had reached America, although without knowing it, and possibly the Amerindians, who would have reached the coasts of Europe, again without knowing what they had discovered. There were other drives, such as those of the universal religions, addressing themselves to all human beings, that spread outward from India to the Far East (Buddhism), from Asia Minor to the West (Christianity), from Arabia to the West, East, and South (Islam). However, the great gods were still quite provincial and ignorant of the Earth, as well as of the humans they were supposed to have created.

Throughout the Western Middle Ages, even though their histories did not communicate with one another, and even though their civilizations remained in hermetic isolation, fruits, vegetables, and domestic animals were transported and introduced from East to West, from Asia to Europe, along with silk, precious stones, and spices. Cherries left the Caspian Sea for Japan and Europe, apricots from China to Persia, and from there to the West. Chickens went from India to all of Eurasia. Harnesses, along with gun powder, paper, and printing, arrived in Europe, as well as the knowledge and instruments necessary for its rise to power, in particular, the discovery of America. Arab civilizations brought the Indian zero to the West. Before modern times, Chinese, Phoenician, Greek, Arab, and Viking navigators discovered the vast spaces of what they did not realize was the planet, and they naively designed maps of the fragment with which they were familiar as though it were the whole world. In the end, western Europe, a little corner of Eurasia, throughout its long Middle Ages, received from the vast Far East the techniques that would allow it to bring together the knowledge and the means to discover and control America.

In this way a multiple transformation, from all parts of the globe, prepared, announced, and produced the instruments and ideas of what would become the Planetary Era. At the very moment the Ottoman empire, after having conquered Byzantium, reached the walls of Vienna and menaced the heart of Europe, the Far West set sail to open the Planetary Era.

1

The Planetary Era

THE PLANETARY REVOLUTION

At the close of the 15th European century, Ming China and Mogul India were the most important civilizations on Earth. Islam, continuing its expansion into Asia and Africa, was the most widespread religion on Earth. The Ottoman Empire, which had expanded from Asia to Eastern Europe, wiped out Byzantium, and threatened Vienna, had become the greatest power in Europe. The Incan and Aztec empires ruled the Americas, and both Tenochtitlan and Cuzco surpassed Madrid, Lisbon, Paris, and London—capitals of young and small West European nations—in terms of population, monuments, and magnificence.

Yet, beginning in 1492, it was these young and small nations that rushed forward to conquer the Globe and, through adventure, war, and death, brought about the Planetary Era.

Following Christopher Columbus, Amerigo Vespucci sighted the continent that now bears his name. At about the same time (1498), Vasco de Gama found the eastern route to the Indies by circumnavigating Africa. In 1521, Magellan's roundtrip voyage proved the roundness of the Earth. In 1521 and 1532, Cortes and

Pizarro discovered the astounding pre-Colombian civilizations, which they proceeded to destroy almost immediately (the Aztec Empire in 1522, the Incan in 1533). During the same period, Copernicus proposed the system in which the planets, including the Earth, rotate on their axes and around the Sun.

Here we have the beginnings of what is called Modern times but which should be called the Planetary Era. The Planetary Era begins with the discovery that the Earth *is* a planet and with the entering into communication among the various parts of the planet.

From the conquest of the Americas to the Copernican revolution, a planet emerged and a cosmos disappeared. The most certain and obvious of worldviews was toppled. The Earth no longer stood at the center of the Universe and became a satellite of the Sun; humanity thus lost its privileged position. The Earth was no longer considered flat but definitively round (the first globe of the Earth appears in Nuremberg in 1492, and in 1526 Magellan's route is inscribed on it). It ceased being thought of as immobile and became a spinning top. The paradise that Columbus sought on Earth was henceforth sought in Heaven or else disappeared altogether. Western Europe discovered great civilizations, as rich and developed as their own, that ignored the God of the Bible along with the message of Christ. China ceased being a strange exception, and Europe had to recognize the plurality of human worlds and the provinciality of the Judeo-Islamo-Christian world.[1]

It would take some time for the implications of such a revolution to sink in. As late as 1632, Gallileo was forced by the Inquisition to recant and condemn the system of Copernicus. Above all, such a revolution would not really revolutionize the West European world that gave birth to it: This world would forget about its provinciality by establishing its dominion over the planet; it would forget about the provinciality of the Earth by convincing itself that science and technology would make it master of the world.

THE BEGINNINGS OF THE PLANETARY ERA

The Planetary Era began with the first microbial and human interactions, along with the vegetable and animal exchanges between the Old and the New Worlds. The Eurasian bacilli and viruses responsible for scarlet fever, herpes, the flu, and tuberculosis ravaged the Amerindians, whereas treponema and syphilis made their way

---

[1]Not only was the Earth no longer thought of as the center of the cosmos, but Europe was no longer the center of the world.

from America to Shanghai. Chance encounters, encounters of desire—and rapes—gave rise to populations of Metis scattered throughout the Americas, where Black Africans captured en masse were brought, at first, to replace the Indians that fell victim to European diseases and merciless colonial exploitation, and later as labor slaves to work the great plantations.

Europeans introduced corn, potatoes, beans, tomatoes, manioc, sweet potatoes, cocoa, and tobacco to their homelands. To America, they brought sheep, cattle, horses, cereal grains, vines, and olive trees, along with tropical plants, rice, yams, coffee, and sugar cane.

Corn, with its superior nutritional value, eventually replaced the oat and millet gruels of Italy and the Balkans. Potatoes brought an end to chronic famine in Central and North Europe, and manioc became Africa's staple food. America built up stock of domesticated herbivores and committed itself to the intensive cultivation of cotton, cane sugar, and coffee.

Maritime commerce, no longer confined to coastal trade, spread across all the seas. The 17th century saw the establishment of the great English, French, and Dutch maritime trading companies in the East and West Indies. Exchanges among Europe, Asia, and America greatly increased, and, in Europe, such exotic luxury items as coffee, chocolate, sugar, and tobacco became products of daily consumption.

Europe underwent an accelerated development. Exchanges intensified. National states built roads and canals. Countries on the Baltic coastline shipped wood, grain, and herring, which they traded for wine and oil from the Mediterranean countries. Ireland and Brittany sold salted meats and butter to the inner provinces. Spain, Germany, and England raised sheep and developed the wool trade. Agriculture was transformed, and leguminous vegetables (peas and clover) fertilized poor soil.

Cities, capitalism, the nation-state, industry, and technology developed at a rate as yet unparalleled by any other civilization. In the midst of wars that were waged against each other—not only in Europe but also in America and Asia—Spain, Portugal, France, the Netherlands, and, as of the 18th century especially, England, developed an awesome economic, maritime, and military power that eventually covered the globe.

The Westernization of the world began in earnest, as much through the immigration of Europeans to the Americas and Australia as through the importing of European civilization—its arms, technologies, and mindset arose in every one of its tradeposts and areas of penetration.

The Planetary Era began with and evolved through violence, destruction, and slavery—the ferocious exploitation of Africa and the Americas. This began the Planetary Iron Age in which we still find ourselves.

THE WESTERNIZATION OF THE WORLD

In the 19th Century, the Planetary Iron Age was marked by the awesome development of European imperialism, mainly British, which procured the mastery of the world. Even though the United States, along with the new nations of Latin America, had already emancipated itself from imperial domination, it did so precisely on the model and according to the norms and values of Western Europe. Thus, through colonialism and emancipation of the colonies, the new phase of the Planetary Era was marked by the Westernization of the world.

In the last decades of the century, although already engaged in a frantic arms race, France, Germany, England, and Russia still did not confront one another directly on their respective homelands. Having at their disposal an absolute technological and military mastery relative to the rest of the world, they preferred to take it out on the world, whose spoils they proceeded to divide among themselves.

At the beginning of the 20th Century, Great Britain controlled all maritime routes worldwide and ruled over India, Ceylon, Singapore, Hong Kong, numerous islands in the West Indies and Polynesia, Nigeria, Rhodesia, Kenya, Uganda, Egypt, the Sudan, Malta, and Gibraltar—in all, one fifth of the world's surface. It numbered some 428 million royal subjects—about one quarter of the world's population. The Netherlands possessed Malaysia, Java, and Borneo. France occupied Algeria, Tunisia, Morocco, Indochina, and a large portion of Black Africa. The Russian Empire extended into Asia all the way to the Pacific and included populations of Turks and Mongols. Germany had built an empire of two and a half million square kilometers, with a population of 14 million, in the southwest of Africa, in Togo, Cameroon, Tanganyika, and in the islands of the Pacific. Italy had taken possession of Somalia, Tripoli, and Eritrea. Belgium had taken the Congo. Portugal had occupied Angola and Mozambique. China had been obliged by the Europeans to make territorial concessions in its great ports and to forego practically the whole of its coastline, from Canton to Tientsin, and had to allow for railways, commercial privileges, and financial opportunities. Only Japan resisted the advances and, using its methods, technology, and arms, inflicted on the white world its first humiliating defeat at Port Arthur in January 1905. In this way Japan contributed to the globalization of Western civilization.

The digging of the Suez and Panama canals freed up traffic between the Atlantic and the Pacific Oceans, the Mediterranean Sea, and the seas of Asia. The Orient Express, Transamerican, and Transiberian railways linked the continents.

Economic development, the development of communications, and the inclusion of subjugated continents into the world market all contributed to the massive population shift, which in turn was amplified by generalized demographic growth.[2] The countryside would populate industrial cities; the wretched and persecuted of Europe would flee to the Americas; adventurers and opportunists would leave for the colonies. In the second half of the 19th century, 9.5 million British, 5 million German, 5 million Italians, and 1 million Scandinavian, Spanish, and inhabitants of the Balkans crossed the Atlantic to the two Americas. There were also migratory flows in Asia, where the Chinese installed themselves as traders in Siam, Java, and the Malay peninsula, and set out for California, British Columbia, New South Wales, and Polynesia, whereas East Indians established themselves in Natal and East Africa.

Imperceptibly, the economy became global. Between 1863 and 1873, multinational commerce, for which London was the capital, became a unified system following the adoption of the gold standard for the currencies of the principal European states. The globality of the market was a globality of competitions and conflicts. It was tied up with the global spread of capitalism and technology, with the globalization of conflict between imperialisms, the globalization of politics, and the global diffusion of the model of the nation-state. Born in Europe, this model would become an instrument of liberation from European domination, a means to safeguard identities threatened by Western modernity, allowing for the appropriation of the arms and means of this modernity. The multiple processes of globalization (demographic, economic, technological, ideological, etc.) were mutually interfering, tumultuous, and conflictual.

---

[2]In one century, Europe went from 190 to 423 million inhabitants, the world from 900 million to 1.6 billion.

THE GLOBALIZATION OF IDEAS

The process of globalization was also evident in the realm of ideas. The universalistic religions were already open in principle to everyone on Earth. From the start of the Planetary Era, the themes of the "noble savage" and of the "natural man" served as antidotes, although admittedly feeble ones, to the arrogance and disdain toward civilized barbarians. In the 18th century, the humanism of the Enlightenment saw all human beings as rational and granted to them an equality of rights. The generalization of the ideas of the French Revolution worked to internalize the principles of the human rights and the sovereignty of the people.

In the 19th century, Darwin's theory of evolution designated all human beings as the descendants of a single primate, and the biological sciences recognized the unity of the human species. However, these universalistic streams were opposed by countercurrents. Although the unity of the human species was recognized, humanity was also compartmentalized into a hierarchy of superior and inferior races. Although the sovereignty of the people was recognized, certain nations considered themselves superior and took upon themselves the mission of guiding or dominating the whole of humanity. Although all human beings were thought to share the same passions and fundamental needs, theorists insisted on the irreducible nature of cultural specificity. Although humanity was everywhere potentially *homo sapiens*, Eurocentrism refused the status of full rationality and adulthood to those it considered "backward," and European anthropology recognized archaic peoples not as "noble savages," but as infantile "primitives."

The fact remains, however, that by the middle of the 19th century, the idea of humanity emerged fully on the scene, styled as a kind of collective being aspiring to realize itself through the reunification of its scattered fragments. August Comte made humanity the mother of every human being. The music of Beethoven, the ideas of Marx, and the works of Hugo and Tolstoy spoke to the whole of humanity. Progress seemed to be the great law of evolution and human history. This progress was guaranteed by developments in science and reason, both of which enjoyed universal applicability. The great promise of universal progress took shape, a promise that was taken up and energized by socialism.

Socialism considered itself as essentially international, and the International took on the mission of uniting the human race. The first International was stillborn, but the second, more powerful International brought together the various socialist parties with the shared agenda of preparing for a world revolution and of putting a stop to all wars.

The Planetary Era was thus also, in the beginning of the 20th century, marked by the aspiration toward the peaceful and brotherly unification of humanity.

GLOBALIZATION THROUGH WAR

The process of globalization, however, becoming more and more tumultuous and conflictual, took another turn. The First World War of 1914-1918 was the first great common denominator to unify humanity. But it unified in death.

At Sarajevo, a Serbian shot and killed the Habsburg heir. The incident occurred in a fractal zone where local nationalisms and worldwide imperialisms interfered and overlapped. The slow decomposition of the Ottoman Empire gave free rein to virulent nationalist forces, stirring up the greediness of the Austro-Hungarians, German, English, and French. The shooting at Sarajevo, in a Bosnia-Herzegovina populated by Serbs, Croats, and Muslims under Habsburg rule, triggered the mobilization of Germany, which triggered the mobilization of France. Germany took the lead by invading Belgium, and dragged all the other powers into the war. In this way a local incident in a lost corner of the Balkans set in motion an explosive chain reaction, which, covering all of Europe, soon involved the colonies of Asia and Africa, as well as Japan, the United States, and Mexico. As the war spread from sea to sea, Canadians, Americans, Australians, Senegalese, Algerians, Moroccans, and Annamites fought on the European front behind the Allied flags.

Thus, it was the centripetal rebound of the rival European imperialisms that brought about the world war. It was the interactions between great imperialisms and small nationalisms that triggered it and exacerbated nationalisms that fed it. It was the chain of cross-alliances and cross-rivalries that drew the rest of the world into war. War had become total, mobilizing entire populations—militarily, economically, and psychologically—ravaging countrysides, destroying cities, bombing civilian populations. The total involvements of nations, progress in automatic arms and artillery, the introduction of mechanized engines of war—of aircraft and, in every ocean, of submarines—would make of it the first great war of mass destruction, in which the planet would lose 8 million human lives.

A veritable historical cyclone was unleashed, drawing into its devastating vortex imperialist interests and nationalist frenzy, along with all the technological and ideological forces unleashed by and throughout the Planetary Iron Age. It would be simplistic to ask whether one could explain the war along Marxist (imperialist rivalries) or Shakespearean (the unleashing of sound and fury, the frenzy of the will to power) lines, for the war was the monstrous historical product of the mad coupling of Marx and Shakespeare.

In this way, Europe, from the top of the world, sunk into the abyss. Its fall opened a new phase in the Planetary Era.

The turmoil did not end in 1918, for, in 1917, a new cyclone emerged out of the first. Internationalism, which was crushed in 1914, took its revenge and profited from the collapse of Tsarist Russia to create, according to Lenin's proudly proclaimed intentions, the first seat of the world revolution. However, the revolution was thwarted in Germany and, apart from a fleeting success in Hungary, failed to take hold in England and France, or anywhere else in the world. Responding to the internationalist revolution of Petrograd and Moscow, and with Germany defeated, there followed the international intervention of the Great Powers: civil war, foreign intervention, famine, and ruin. The anemic Bolshevik state held on to the territories of Tsarist Russia after war and hunger killed 13 million people; it established a regime with communist goals that covered one sixth of the globe. However, through its victory, it created a new and monstrous political entity, born of the subjection of the modern state to a hypercentralized party and having a worldwide reach: totalitarianism.

Reacting to communism, the nationalisms intensified and, in a frustrated, prerevolutionary Italy, a second form of totalitarianism—fascism—emerged. Fascism is identical to communist totalitarianism in its single-party system, but antagonistic in its nationalist ideology. The U.S.S.R, for its part, was progressively and surreptitiously penetrated from within by nationalism and imperialism.

The planetary convulsions, begun in 1914 and renewed in 1917, did not cease but continued to affect one another in sequence.

In the early 1920s, the world economy was unstable until, in the middle of a regained prosperity, the great crisis of 1929 revealed, through disaster, a worldwide economic solidarity: a crash on Wall Street spread an economic depression to all the continents. After two years of crisis, a quarter of the industrialized countries' workforce found itself unemployed.

The effects of the First World War, the Bolshevik revolution, and the world economic crisis combined and concentrated in

Germany, where, in 1931, the shockwave from Wall Street hit with extreme brutality. The suffering and distress of unemployment revived the sense of national humiliation caused by the Treaty of Versailles, and the fear of "stateless" communism inflamed the desire for nationalist revenge and the hatred of the Jews, cast by Hitler as diabolical manipulators of an international plutocratic/bolshevik plot. The National Socialist German Worker's Party (NSDAP), which concentrated in its name nationalist malignancies and socialist aspirations, came legally to power in 1933, and proceeded without delay to set up the totalitarian single-party system. Its ideology of the superiority of the Aryan race awakened a pan-Germanic imperialism and egged on Nazi Germany to dominate the whole of Europe.

The 1930s were dramatic. New storms broke on the planet. The Japanese army invaded China and began a war that would last until 1945, extending to civil war up to 1949. Everywhere, at the heart of the crisis, fascist and revolutionary elements collided, provoking riots, street fights, and, in Spain, civil war. Except for the United States and England, all democracies revealed their vulnerability. The refurbishing of the German war machine restimulated a generalized arms race, which neutralized the economic crisis—although most countries still had more than 10% unemployment. Stalinist communism revealed its horror at the Moscow trials, and Hitlerian Nazism horrified no less in its concentration camps, the ghettoization and stigmatization of the Jews, and the physical liquidation of Rohm and the SA. Disoriented by the rising dangers, unable to believe in an impotent democracy, many wavered between fascism and Stalinism, not knowing which of the two was the lesser evil. Remilitarized Germany annexed Austria, imposed its claims on the Sudetes Mountains (which it captured), subjugated Czechoslovakia, reclaimed Danzig, and invaded Poland. The Second World War began in September 1939.

In 1940, Nazi Germany invaded Norway, Holland, Belgium, France, and, flanked by Mussolini's Italy, domesticated or invaded the rest of Europe (1940-1941), with the exception of Spain, Turkey, Portugal, Switzerland, and parts of Sweden. The war became truly global with the German attack on the U.S.S.R., the Japanese attack at Pearl Harbor (December 1941), the war in Libya and Egypt, naval war on all the oceans, and the spread of aerial bombing over all nations in conflict, leading to the destruction of the Third Reich at Berlin in May 1945 and the annihilation of Hiroshima and Nagasaki in August of the same year.

Of the 100 million men and women engaged in the world conflict, 15 million soldiers and 35 million civilians were killed. The two U.S. atomic bombs released over Hiroshima and Nagasaki alone claimed 72,000 dead and 80,000 wounded, ending the global massacre with a crescendo.

FROM HOPE TO THE DAMOCLEAN THREAT

Great hopes for a new world, for peace and justice, took shape with the death of Nazism, by forgetting or with the ignorance that the Red Army did not bring liberation but another form of servitude, and that colonialism had reasserted its hold in Africa and Asia. The United Nations, instituted by the coalition of victors, was soon paralyzed by the rapid crystallization of the world into two camps about to enter into conflict on all points of the globe.

The Cold War began in 1947. The planet was thus polarized into two blocks, both of which were caught up in an unremitting ideological war. Despite the mutuality of atomic terror, the world was nevertheless far from stable. East-West bipolarization, from 1946 to 1989, in no way prevented enormous collapses, uprisings, and transformations all over the world. The face of the planet was altered with the dislocation and liquidation of the colonial empires, which sometimes came about at the price of relentless wars (e.g., the two Vietnam wars, the Algerian war). The Third World emerged in the guise of new nations, sometimes comprising heterogeneous ethnic groups, which gave rise to new problems (oppression of minorities, religious rivalries), and where, apart from a few great federations, as with India or Malaysia, an artificial balkanization separated complimentary territories. These nations were torn between East and West, that is, between two recipes for development that, instead of solutions, more often than not brought with them military or totalitarian dictatorships, corruption, exploitation, and the degradation of indigenous cultures. An attempt at a neutral third way took shape in Bandung (April, 1955), headed by India, Egypt, and Yugoslavia, but here again there was dislocation and failure.

Throughout these years, populous China, Vietnam, and Cuba escaped the Occidental orbit and joined the "socialist camp." Egypt, Iraq, and Syria changed and exchanged camps. Following the formation of the state of Israel, the Middle East became a zone of fractures and pestilence for the whole world. The Cold War turned into chronic belligerences, with periodic flare-ups of real wars (the Sinai War of 1956, the Six Day War of 1967, the Yom Kippur War of 1973, the Lebanese War of 1975). The Middle East manifested the first confrontations between Christians, Moslems, and Jews, and between tradition and modernity, East and West, secular and religious, along with the concentration of enormous conflicts of interest regarding the appropriation and control of oil.

The giant Communist block, united by the "eternal and indefectible friendship" between the U.S.S.R. and China, split in 1960. A new cold war separated the two ex-sister republics, tempting Brejnev's U.S.S.R. to use the atomic bomb against Mao's China.

Apart from a few passing bright spots, the antagonism between the two great systems maintained its virulence up to 1985 and became exacerbated during the Afghanistan war, during which time the collisions intensified between secularism and religion, East and West, North and South, modernity and fundamentalism. An ideological abyss seemed to have stifled all hope for a better future.

From 1956 to 1970, the hope for the revolutionary messiah shifted from the U.S.S.R. to China and rekindled in Vietnam and Cuba. However, after the fading of the myth of "socialist realism," which began with the Krutchev report, followed by the repression of the Hungarian revolution (1957) and the Prague Spring (1968), the myth of Chinese socialism, for its part, began its decline in 1975 (the Lin Piao conspiracy, the affair of the Gang of Four), along with the myth of Vietnam the Liberator (the subjugation of Cambodia) and that of Free Cuba. Finally, with the reforming process of *perestroika*, which resulted in the implosion of totalitarian communism and the dislocation of its empire (1987-1991), came the collapse of the great religion of earthly salvation, which during the 19th century evolved to suppress the mutual exploitation of human beings, and which the 20th forged through the abominable trials of the two World Wars with the hope of ending all wars, along with all human-wrought oppression and distress.

There came about an apparent triumph of Western models: democracy, market economy, and free enterprise. However, the collapse of Eastern totalitarianism did not long mask the problems that beset the West's economy, society, and civilization, nor did it in any way reduce the problems of the Third World—which had become the Southern World—and in no way brought about a peaceful world order.

The invasion of Kuwait and the Gulf War (1991-1992) proved that the Middle East remains a fault line for the entire world. The war between Armenians and Azeris showed that this line extends to the North, crossing over into the ex-Soviet Union, and the Moslem uprisings in North Africa—notably those in Algeria—proved that the line extends West to the Mediterranean. As of 1991, moreover, new historical tornadoes were in process of forming.

The decomposition of totalitarianism triggered a triple crisis in all countries of the former Soviet empire: (a) a political crisis—born of the democratic fragility and inadequacy of the new regimes and gangrened by the bureaucracies and mafias that maintain continuity with the old system, often headed by brutal ex-aparatchiks turned hypernationalists so as better to ride the incoming waves; (b) an economic crisis—resulting from transitional impoverishment, uncertainty, and disorder that threaten to persist, caught between an old system that, although spurned, provided a minimum standard of living and safety and a new system that has yet to deliver any of the hoped for benefits; and (c) a nationalist crisis—aggravated by the eruption of ethnocentrisms and particularisms and the return of sometimes millenarian hatreds resurrected by problems with minorities and boundaries. These crises are mutually stimulating. Disorder and hardship, linked with nationalist exasperation, favor the appearance of new dictatorships, whether military or "populist," and transform territorial dissociations into armed conflicts, as has already happened in Moldavia, Armenia-Azerbaidjan, Georgia, and the former Yugoslavia.

The convulsions of the post-communist period accelerated and amplified a formidable process of return to the past—to tradition, religion, and ethnicity. This return is born, to a certain extent all over the world, from the crisis of the future (see Chapter 3) and the threat to local identities of increasing homogenization. The defense of cultural identities is anti-hegemonic, anti-homogenizing, decentralizing, and favors greater autonomy. To the extent that it is integrated within a wider, associative framework, this defense appears to be a healthy phenomenon. At the same time, however, the dislocation and disintegration of empires and polyethnic nations, in the frenetic race of each ethnic group toward absolute political sovereignty, is a threat to the very future of the planet. In fact, a multifaceted world struggle is now in process, continuing to the end of the century and perhaps beyond, between the forces of association and dissociation, of integration and disintegration. The struggle is random and the future radically uncertain. What is certain is that history has again taken up its riotous march and is heading toward an unknown future as it strives to return to a vanished past.

Furthermore, in 1945, the bomb on Hiroshima brought the Planetary Iron Age into a Damoclean phase. Fear of the nuclear threat, although temporarily assuaged, has been reawakened over the last decade. As the United States and Russia attempt to reduce a nuclear stockpile capable of destroying humanity several times over, weapons are being miniaturized and more widely disseminated. They are already in the hands of paranoid states and will soon be made available to insane dictators and terrorist groups. Humanity must henceforth live with the possibility of its self-destruction.

Another Damoclean threat has arisen since the ecological alert of 1970-1972: We have become increasingly aware, throughout the 1980s, of how technoindustrial development gives rise to many forms of pollution and environmental degradation. Death itself hovers in the air with the Greenhouse Effect. With these threats, a new kind of death has been introduced into the sphere of life of which humanity is a part.

ECONOMIC GLOBALIZATION

Through a worldwide dialogical process between the forces of integration and disintegration on all levels—cultural, social, psychological, and political—economic activity itself has become more and more global and equally fragile. Thus, the economic crisis of 1973, born of a shortage of oil, went through many ups and downs without ever really being solved.

The global economy is increasingly manifesting the nature of an interdependent whole: Each of its parts has become dependent on the whole and, in a reciprocal manner, the whole is influenced by the perturbations and chance happenings that influence the parts.

The drop in market prices for coffee, for example, encourages Colombian peasants to cultivate coca, which will supply the global networks of drug processing and trade, as well as of money laundered in the banks of countries such as Switzerland. By the same token, a 5% rise in salaries in Germany can effect the cocoa trade on the Ivory Coast by means of a general slowing down of economic activity: (a) the rise incites the Central Bank, which fears inflation, to restrain liquidities and raise the interest rate; (b) the Bank of France follows suit to avoid a flight of capital to Germany; (c) Japanese funds are invested in Germany; (d) the United States, short of money, raises its interest rate; (e) consumption decreases everywhere on the planet, which slows down economic activity; (f) Third World countries, whose interest rates are indexed, must make larger payments on their debts; and g) there is less demand for exports from underdeveloped countries, so raw materials, including cocoa from the Ivory Coast, must sell at lowered prices.

Economic globalization both unifies and divides, equalizes and inequalizes. Economic developments in the West and East Asia tend toward a local reduction in inequalities. On a global scale, however, there is increasing inequality between the "developed" nations (where 20% of the world's population consumes 80% of world production) and those that remain underdeveloped.

THE HOLOGRAM

Not only is it the case that every part of the world is more and more party to the world, but the world as a whole is more and more present in each of the parts. This truth is evident not only for nations and peoples but for individuals as well. Just as each point on a hologram contains information about the whole of which it is a part, so each individual henceforth takes in or assimilates matter and information from everywhere in the world.

Thus, a European man wakens each morning to turn on his Japanese radio, which tells of events from around the world: Volcanic eruptions, earthquakes, coups, and international conferences are piped into the room while he sips tea from Ceylon, India, or China, or perhaps mocha coffee from Ethiopia or an arabica from Latin America. He lingers in a bubble bath with oils from Tahiti, then makes use of exotically scented aftershave. He puts on a sweater, underpants, and a shirt made of cotton from Egypt or India, pants and jacket made from Australian wool, treated in Manchester and Roubaix-Tourcoing, or perhaps a leather jacket from China with American jeans. His watch is Swiss or Japanese. His glasses have tortoise shell from the Galapagos Islands. His wallet is of Caribbean peccary or of some African reptile. He might have on his dining table strawberries and cherries from Argentina or Chile in the middle of Winter, along with green beans from Senegal, avocados or pineapples from Africa, and melons from Martinique, Russian vodka, Mexican tequila, American bourbon, and Irish beer. He can listen at home to a German symphony with a Korean conductor or watch a performance of *La Bohème* on television with the black singer Barbara Hendricks as Mimi and the Spaniard Placido Domingo as Rudolph.

The African woman in her shantytown, although not included in this planetary network of comfort, is nevertheless equally part of the planetary network. Her daily life is prey to the ups and downs of the world market, which set the price of cocoa, sugar, and other raw materials that her country produces. She has been chased out of the village by global processes originating in the West, most notably by the development of industrialized monocultures. She has gone from being a self-sufficient peasant to being a suburban city-dweller in search of a salary. Her needs are henceforth calculated in monetary terms. She aspires to a decent standard of living. She uses aluminum or plastic cookware, drinks beer or Coca-Cola. She sleeps on salvaged sheets of polystyrene and wears T-shirts with American prints. She dances to syncretistic tunes that incorporate rhythms from her native tradition within an American orchestration that echoes the memory of her enslaved ancestors' contribution. This African, now an object of the world market, has also become the subject of a state organized along Western lines. Thus, for better or worse, whether rich or poor, every one of us harbors within him- or herself, for the most part unknowingly, the entire planet. The fact of globalization is at once evident, subconscious, and omnipresent.

INDICATIONS OF A PLANETARY CONSCIOUSNESS

Despite all the regressions and the generalized unconsciousness, there now exist, in this latter half of the 20th century, indications of a planetary consciousness.

The Persistence of a Global Nuclear Threat

The nuclear threat was and remains a factor of the new planetary consciousness. The great and malignant fear of 1945-1962, anesthetized by the balance of terror, is reawakening. A new time of troubles has replaced the old, and nuclear arms are once again a global threat to humanity through their miniaturization and dissemination to new nation-states.

The Emergence of a Planetary Ecological Consciousness

The object of the science of ecology is increasingly coinciding with the biosphere as a whole and as a function of the multiplication of the types of environmental degradation and pollution on every continent, and finally, as of 1980, as a result of the detection of a global threat to all life on the planet. Out of this has arisen a growing consciousness, made explicit in Rio in 1992, of the vital necessity on the part of all of humanity to safeguard the integrity of the Earth (for more on planetary ecology, see Chapter 3).

The World Recognizes the Third World

With the process of decolonization between 1950 and 1960, 1.5 billion human beings, who until that time had been repressed by the West into the depths of history, suddenly appeared on the world scene. Two thirds of the world, which we call the Third World, finally became part of the world. Whether this portion of humanity inspires fear or compassion, its tragedies, its frustrated needs, its sheer mass impel us constantly to relativize our Western problems, to globalize our perception and conception of things human. In point of fact, the problems of the Third World (demography, nutrition, development) are increasingly being recognized as the problems of the entire world as such.

Along with, and despite, its many ethnocentric divisions, the Planetary Era enjoins us to recognize at once the unity of humanity and the specific interests of the cultures that have diversified this unity. This recognition has been facilitated by the availability of anthropological studies by the likes of Levi-Strauss, Malaurie, Clastre, and Jaulin, and of documentaries or films such as *Les Hommes d'Aran, Ombres blanches, Naviouk,* or *Dersou Ouzala.* Little by little, the Western point of view, which has considered as backward human beings from non-Western societies, and as infantile those from archaic societies, is awakening to a new, more open perception that acknowledges their shrewdness and know-how along with the incredible richness and diversity of the world's cultures.

The Development of Global Civilization

We are witnessing, for better or worse, the development of a global civilization: for the worse—such a development brings irremediable cultural destruction in its train. It homogenizes and standardizes mores, customs, patterns of consumption, food (fast food), travel, and tourism. Yet this global civilization also works for the better insofar as it provides customs, mores, and common lifestyles that cross national, ethnic, and religious boundaries and work to lift a certain number of barriers to mutual comprehension between individuals and peoples. It develops vast sectors of secularity and rationality in which religious prohibitions and maledictions no longer hold sway. Communication among adolescents, who share the same aspirations, the same codes and cosmopolitan culture, is also on the rise. Engineers, scientists, and business people, for their part, circulate throughout networks of international relations, colloquia, congresses, and seminars. One must not, however, lose sight of the countercurrents that, by secularizing national and ethnic identity, reinstate the old barriers and rejections. Here again, the same process involves a profound ambivalence.

The Globalization of Cultures

Although the notion of civilization includes everything that is essentially universal—technologies, utility goods, know-how, and lifestyles based on the use and consumption of these technologies and goods—the notion of culture includes everything that is unique, specific, and original to a given ethnic group or nation. The contents of these two notions, however, are to a certain extent interchangeable. I have indicated elsewhere (Morin, 1987) that science, technology, nationality, and secularity were all historical products peculiar to Western culture before becoming elements of civilization that were subsequently universalized. The spread of this civilization, generalizing new modes of life and ways of thinking, ends up creating a cosmopolitan culture—the culture of the Planetary Era.

Cultural development is an ambivalent process consisting of two antagonistic aspects: (a) homogenization, degradation, loss of diversity; and (b) encounters, new syntheses, new diversity.

With regard to art, music, literature, and thought, the globalization of cultures is not homogenizing. It consists of great transnational waves that nevertheless foster in their midst the expression of national originality. Such was the case in Europe with Classicism, the Enlightenment, Romanticism, Realism, and Surrealism. The mutual translation of novels, essays, and philosophical works allowed each country access to the works of other countries and enabled them to feed from a common European culture, which they in turn fed with their own works. The 20th century brought about the globalization of this cultural process. Translations multiply. Japanese, Latin American, and African novels are published in the European languages, and European novels are published in Asia and the Americas. To be sure, this new global culture, which gathers together the original contributions of multiple cultures, is still confined to restricted spheres in each nation, but its development is a distinctive trait of the second part of the 20th century.

In a parallel fashion, oriental cultures arouse the curiosity and interest of the West. The *Avesta* and the *Upanishads* had already been translated in the 18th century, Confucius and Lao Tzu in the 19th, but the teachings of the East remained the exclusive domain of erudite studies. It is only during the 20th century that the philosophies and mysticism of Islam, the sacred texts of India, and Taoist and Buddhist thought became vital resources for the Western soul, drawn to and fettered by ceaseless activity and productivity, efficiency, and distraction. Thus, for instance, one now sees a growing demand for popularized and commercialized forms of yoga and Zen that promise harmony for the body and peace for the soul.

The Formation of a Planetary Folklore

Throughout this century, the media have produced, broadcasted, and churned a global folklore on the basis of original themes from various cultures, sometimes nativized, sometimes syncretized. It all began during the 1920s with the movies, which, as the academician Georges Duhamel put it, expressing the disdain of the intellectuals and academics, were first looked on as "entertainment for Helots." The movies became the stuff of art as much as industry—a paradox that long remained unintelligible to the high intelligentsia—then, following a time spent in Purgatory, were thereafter recognized as the seventh art. Hollywood's formidable "dream factory" created and propagated a new global folklore with Westerns, Mysteries, Thrillers, Musicals, and animated films from Walt Disney to Tex Avery. Western and Eastern nations produced their own films. To be sure, there is often more fascination than creation in a great number of films, but the wonder is that the art of the film flourished on all the continents and that, with dubbing and television broadcasting, it became a global art form that managed to preserve the original contributions of the respective artists and cultures. One could even say that co-productions, from Visconti's *Leopard* to Kurosawa's *Ran*, which bring together directors, actors, and artists of different nationalities, as often happens nowadays, attain through the cosmopolitan nature of their production an esthetic authenticity that is lost in impoverished regional folklores.

A planetary folklore has been constituted and enriched through integrations and encounters. It took jazz from New Orleans and, branching out in a variety of styles, spread it all over the world. The same happened with the tango, born in the harbor district of Buenos Aires, and the Cuban mambo, the Viennese waltz, and especially American rock, which has produced a whole spectrum of styles the world over. This folklore has integrated the Indian sitar of Ravi Shankar, Andalousian flamenco, the Arab chanting of Oum Kalsoum, and the Andean huayno. It has given rise to the syncretisms of salsa, raï, and flamenco rock.

The development of cultural globalization is obviously inseparable from the global development of media networks, along with the global dissemination of reproduction technology (cassettes, CDs, videos).

Planetary Teleparticipation

Wars in Asia were totally ignored in Europe up until the 20th century. The invasion of China by Japan in 1931 was very peripheral and far away, known only through a few dated newsreels. The Chaco war between Bolivia and Argentina (1932-1935) happened on another planet. It is only after 1950, with the general availability of television, that the wars in Korea, Vietnam, and the Middle East were brought closer to home.

Since then, the world enters our homes every evening at dinner time, seen as through a kaleidoscope, with images of floods, cyclones, lava or mud flows, famines, murders, palace revolutions, terrorism, international games, and world championships. There is no major event, happening, or catastrophe that is not caught on camera and sent to all horizons in hundreds of millions of snapshots. The world had live coverage of the assassination of President Kennedy in Dallas in 1963, then the assassination of his alleged assassin, the arrival of Sadat in Jerusalem and his assassination in 1981, the assassination attempt against the Pope at Saint Peter's in Rome, the assassination of Indira Gandhi and that of her son Rhaju who had succeeded her, Boris Yeltsin on top of a tank, defying the leaders of the Moscow Putsch, the landing of Mikhail Gorbatchev's plane after his sequestration, and the assassination in the Anaba Cultural Center of Mohammed Boudiaf. Since 1991, CNN scans the world daily, seeking out with its camera gaze any newsworthy event on all points of the globe. It installed us in Baghdad during the American bombing and in Tel Aviv during the interception of Scuds by the Patriots. It found us a place in Clinton's investiture train.

What a bizarre phenomenon, this process of globalization: We consume, as mere spectators, the tragedies, hecatombs, and horrors of this world, but we also participate in other people's lives and are moved by their misfortune. If only for the duration of a news flash, human emotions are stirred and people are moved to donate clothes or contribute to international relief agencies and humanitarian missions.

It is true that, even at the beginning of this century, there were charity bazaars or philanthropic collections to feed the "little Chinese." Yet the misfortunes of the world were neither seen nor heard by the West. For a long time, moreover, the war of ideologies made us deaf and blind to the tortures committed for the sake of the good cause. The crack in the wall of indifference first appeared in 1969-1970 with the arrival in Biafra of physicians without ideological boundaries. Today we are interested in, and commiserate with, other peoples' hardships because we see them (but only when we see them).[3] Thus, food and medical supplies make their way to distant lands of affliction.

---

[3]Thus, the hecatombs of the Nazi camps were only acknowledged with the arrival on the premises of the Allied troops, the millions who died in the Gulag were ignored for decades, and the horrors of the Chinese Cultural Revolution remained mute. There are today, as there shall be tomorrow, zones of suffering and terror that will stay hidden or ignored because no television camera is present to tell us otherwise.

In this way, a planetary teleparticipation has constituted itself: Catastrophes that strike our antipodes give rise to fleeting transports of compassion and the feeling of belonging to the same community of destiny, which henceforth is the community of planet Earth. If only for the duration of a news flash, we feel we are part of the planet. Such is McLuhan's "global village"—united and divided like a village, beset with incomprehension and enmity like a village.

The Earth Seen from the Earth

Planet Earth has recently revealed itself to the gaze of Earthlings. Following the first Sputnik of 1957 and the first circumplanetary flight by the Magellan of space, Yuri Gagarin, a large portion of humanity was able to contemplate, in 1969, on television screens, the Earth seen from the moon. From that point on, the planetary presence, spread about and multiplied by the press, posters, and T-shirts, found a home in each of us.

Despite particularist, local, and ethnocentric fixations, despite the incapacity to contextualize problems (which one finds not only among isolated peasants, but among abstract technocrats as well), despite the fragmentary perceptions, the sense that there is a planetary entity to which we all belong, and that there are problems of a global nature, is becoming more concrete. In multiple fashion, although still intermittently, we are witnessing an evolution toward a planetary consciousness or global mind

THE SURGE OF HUMANITY

To the ancient bioanthropological substrate that constitutes the unity of the human species is henceforth added a communicational, civilizational, cultural, economic, technological, intellectual, and ideological fabric. The human species henceforth takes the form of humanity. From now on, humanity and the planet can manifest themselves in their unity, which is not only a physical and biospheric, but a historical unity: that of the Planetary Era.

Migrations and interracial couplings—producers of new, polyethnic, and polycultural societies—seem to represent the Homeland common to us all. Nevertheless, the formidable mixings of populations are more given to juxtaposition and hierarchization than to true integration. In the meeting of cultures, there is still more misunderstanding than understanding; along with a gradual osmosis, there are strong forces of rejection. Globalism is on the rise, but we are just waking up to the fact.

Despite increasing communication, humanity is still something of a patchwork. Balkanization is proceeding apace with globalization (see Chapter 3). There are embryos of planetary thought and practice, but there are also numerous setbacks and paralyses as a result of localisms and provincialisms. The intersolidary unity of the planet has not become a social unity (a society of nations), and, although there is henceforth a community of destiny, there is not yet a common consciousness of this *Schicksalgemeinshaft*.

On the contrary, just as in the first part of the 20th century, planetary interdependence was revealed by two world wars, so the progress of planetization, in this turn of the millennium, is revealing itself in convulsive struggles.

2

Citizens of the Earth

From 1950-1970, ideas that appeared to be most assured about the nature of the universe, about the nature of the Earth, about the nature of Life, and even about human nature were overthrown by concomitant advances made in astrophysics, the sciences of the Earth, biology, and paleontology. These revolutionizing advances opened the way for the rise of a new planetary consciousness.

FROM COSMOS TO COSMOS

For millenia, the universe was centered on a queenly Earth, around which the Sun and planets traced their obedient orbits. Ancient astronomers had sighted this world; Ptolemy had confirmed it in his system, a system held to be valid up to the beginning of modern times.

Then, with Copernicus, Kepler, and Galileo, the Earth was no longer at the center of the universe and became a spherical planet circling the Sun, just like the other planets. Yet the Sun remained at the center of everything. Up to the end of the 18th century, the universe continued to follow a faultless order, which witnessed to the perfection of its divine Creator. Newton had set the laws that directed the ballet of bodies that make up the harmonious celestial mechanism. At the start of the 19th century, Laplace cast out the Creator God from a self-sufficient universe to become forever a perfect machine. Furthermore, up to the start of the 20th century, the universe remained faultlessly static. Even after it had been deprived by Einstein of any privileged center, it remained stamped with uncreatedness, self-sufficiency, and infinite duration.

It was only during 1923 that astronomy discovered the existence of other galaxies, soon to be numbered in the millions, and that therefore marginalized our own. In 1929, the red shift of far away galactic light, as evidenced by Hubble, provided the first empirical indication of an expanding universe. Galaxies move away from each other within a universal drift that attains terrific speeds and, following this debacle, the eternal order of the universe collapses.

This expanding and dispersive universe will endure an even greater cataclysm during the second half of the 20th century. In 1965, Penzias and Wilson picked up isotropic radiation coming from all horizons of the universe. This "cosmic background noise" could not be explained except as the fossil residue of an initial deflagration, and the hypothesis of a universe expanding and spreading as a result of a primal catastrophe began to take shape (see Ferris, 1988). It was at once supposed that an initial *fiat lux* had given rise to the universe in the form of radiation attaining 10^{11} degrees K, and that, in one millionth of a second, photons, quarks, electrons, and neutrinos had been created. Then, in the intensive thermic agitation in which a progressive cooling down was beginning, nuclei and atoms of hydrogen were formed by particles colliding. There remained to understand how, in this homogeneous primitive universe, the first disparities had appeared that alone could account for its breakup into unequal metagalaxies, mothers of galaxies and stars. This information was obtained in April 1992 by the Cobe satellite, which detected at the borders of the universe, 15 billion light years distant, infinitesimal variations in the density of matter dating back possibly to only 300,000 years after the original event.[1]

In the 1960s, at the same time that this prodigious history of the cosmos was being revealed, undreamt of things began to appear in the universe: Quasars (1963), pulsars (1968), black holes, and astrophysicists' calculations led to the view that we know only 10% of matter, 90% remaining as yet invisible to our detecting instruments.

[1]Interpreted then as residues from the inception of heterogenization in the distribution of matter—the prelude to the formation of galaxies.

We exist, accordingly, in a universe that consists only to a very limited degree of stars and planets, and that harbors enormous quantities of invisible, "dark" matter.

Here we are, at the turn of the millennium, in a universe that, from its very beginnings, contains the Unknowable, the Unfathomable, and the Inconceivable. Here we are in a universe born of disaster and that could only be organized thanks to an infinitesimal imperfection and to a stupendous destruction (antimatter). Here we are in a universe that is self-created, self-made, and self-organizing, having started with an event/accident that escapes all our present intellectual abilities. Here we are in a universe of which the ecosystem, required by its organization, is apparently nothingness (every self-organizing reality feeds on energies; our universe feeds on the awesome energies born from the initial thermic outburst; but where do these energies come from?). Here we are in a universe that gets organized through disintegration.

Furthermore, there are other stunning mysteries, among which is the annihilation of antiparticles at the very moment of their formation—that is, the almost complete destruction of antimatter by matter, unless, as stunningly and as mysteriously, a universe of antimatter matches our universe in some hidden fashion, or again unless our universe is but a branch of a polymorphic pluriverse. Here we are in a universe verging on the impossible, which, if deprived of the precisely defined density of its matter, would either have had to shrink again as soon as it was born, or would have expanded without producing galaxies or stars. Here we are in a universe of galaxies bumping into each other, of heavenly bodies colliding and exploding, in which the star, no more a spherical beacon in the sky, is a slow-motion hydrogen bomb, a motor of flames. Here we are in a universe in which chaos is at work and that patterns its action through a dialogue between order and disorder, which, although natural enemies, are also accomplices, giving rise to galactic, stellar, nuclear, and atomic organizations. Here we are in a universe whose riddles will certainly be solved, at least in part, but that will never regain its ancient mechanical simplicity, that will never regain its solar center, and in which other phenomena will appear, more stunning still than those we have just discovered.

Furthermore, here we are in a marginal galaxy, the Milky Way, formed 8 billion years after the birth of the universe, and which, together with its neighbors, seems to be drawn to a huge invisible mass called the "Great Attractor." Here we are orbiting around a minor subject of the Milky Way empire, formed 13 billion years after the birth of the universe, 5 billion years after the Milky Way, on a small planet born 4 billion years ago.

Although recently discovered, all of this is known today, and although widely diffused by books, newspapers, and the TV expositions of Hawking and Reeves, the new cosmos has not penetrated our minds, which live still at the center of the universe, on a static Earth, and under an eternal Sun. These new facts have not aroused any curiosity, astonishment, or reflection among most professional philosophers, including those who deal with the world. The reason is that our philosophy has sterilized the astonishment from which it was born. Our education has taught us to separate, to compartmentalize, to isolate, and not to join notions together; therefore, it makes us conceive our humanity as an island, outside the cosmos that surrounds us, outside the physical matter of which we are constituted.

Thus we know, without wanting to know, that we arose from this world, that all our particles were formed 15 billion years ago, that our carbon atoms were constituted in a sun anterior to ours, that our molecules were born on Earth, unless they arrived here by way of meteorites. We know without wanting to know that we are children of this cosmos, the carrier of our birth, of our life, and of our death.

That is why we do not know as yet how to stand within it, how to join together our questions about the universe and our questions about ourselves. We do not feel like thinking about our physical and earthly destiny. We have not yet drawn inferences from the marginal, peripheral situation of our lost planet and from our situation on this planet.

Yet it is in the cosmos that we must locate our planet and our destiny, our meditations, ideas, longings, fears, and decisions.

A UNIQUE PLANET

What is this planet, this cosmic speck of dust where life has emerged; where plants have produced the oxygen of its atmosphere; where living beings as a whole, spreading all over its surface, have constituted a self-organizing and self-regulating biosphere; where, branching off from the animal world, the adventure of hominization continues to unfold?

This cosmic speck of dust is a world, albeit unknown for a long time to the very people who, although living separately from one another, had covered the planet for many tens of thousands of years. The systematic exploration of the Earth's surface has taken place contemporaneously with the unfolding of the Planetary Era and has banished paradise, titans, giants, and gods or other fabulous beings to see in their place an Earth of plants, animals, and humans. From the 18th century on, scientific investigations have penetrated the Earth's surface and begun the study of the physical nature of the planet (geology), the nature of its elements (chemistry), and the mysterious nature of its fossils (paleontology). The Earth not only has a surface, it also has depths. It is no longer static, but evolutive. A discovery was made: The Earth has a history.[2] This history took shape during the 19th century.[3] Early in the 20th century, German scientist Alfred Wegener elaborated on the theory of continental drift, which, after much opposition, was gradually confirmed thanks to a systematic exploration of the ocean floor, from 1950 on, using the techniques of magnetic, electric, seismic, and acoustic soundings.

A new cosmos, together with a new Earth, appeared during the 1960s. Plate tectonics made it possible to link together the sciences of the Earth in a coordinated fashion, and the planet, no longer a ball, a prop, or a pedestal, became a complex being with a life of its own and its own history. This being is also a thermal machine that incessantly reorganizes itself. The crust or bark covers the mantle, a kind of soft-boiled egg, beneath which is a core where excessive heat holds sway.

Our crust has experienced and will go on experiencing stupendous adventures made of dissociative and reassociative movements, both vertical and horizontal, of drifts, collisions, shocks (earthquakes), short-circuits (volcanic eruptions), catastrophic impacts from huge meteorites, and periods of glaciation and thaw.

Where did the Earth come from? In the last decades of this century, its genesis is no longer conceived in terms of a divorce from the Sun, but as a gathering of celestial detritus (Allègre, 1992). In this view, it took shape like the other planets, thanks to the concourse and conglomeration of cosmic dust, perhaps following the explosion of a supernova and the ensuing constitution of "planetesimals," which met and agglomerated in the very movement

---

[2]Giovanni Arduino (1759), an Italian, classified rocks into three periods: primary, secondary, and tertiary. Buffon (1774-1778) tackled a first chronology of the whole globe, starting with the birth of our planet, supposedly a fragment snatched from the Sun by a comet. He considered its physical, zoological, botanical, and finally anthropological processes, asserting that "human life . . . is but a dot on the time continuum."

[3]The notion of syncline, but forward by James Dana (1873), an American naturalist, made it possible to understand reliefs as due to a process of folding. Edouard Suess (1875), an Austrian geologist, explained sea regressions and transgressions by ocean level variations. The American geologist Dutton, in 1889, formulated the isostatic theory of the Earth's crust, floating on a fluid core.

whereby the solar system was formed. The pregnant Earth then became a satellite of the newborn Sun; this very heterogeneous conglomerate structured itself into a core and mantle, and, issuing from the mantle, a thick magma solidified to form the crust.

The Earth is a chaotic being whose organization constituted itself in the midst of the confrontation/collaboration of order and disorder. Its childhood was subjected to bombardment by meteorites and to gas-spitting eruptions. These gases produced water and the first atmosphere, while iron flowed toward the center where it remained as liquid. Then, still in the midst of eruptions and earthquakes, storms broke out at temperatures reaching 250 degrees. Diluvial waters brought about the first erosions, fostered the formation of limestone (calcium catching the carbonic gas of the atmosphere), and occasioned a lowering of the temperature.

From its birth to 2.7 billion years ago, the Earth remained very active, geologically speaking, destroying and transforming the first emerged/immersed marks of its history. This archaic period is probably when the first continents took shape, soon to be intensively eroded.

About 560 million years ago, the Earth entered a kind of extended Middle Age during which the archaic crust was replaced by a new one made of sediments that were hardened, folded, eroded, and consolidated by the intrusion of granites—a patchwork that broke up into continents drifting away from each other. The theory of plate tectonics makes it possible today to fathom the complex phenomenon of the construction of the Earth's surface, whereby it obtained its present-day appearance, after 2 billion years during which life developed and expanded. In this way, a heap of cosmic rubbish has taken shape and organization in the process of becoming planet Earth, and, in the midst of a 4 billion-year turbulent adventure, it has formed and organized for itself a complex system with a core, a mantle, and a crust.

There it is—a planet apparently made wiser, with its continents, islands, mountains, valleys, landscapes; its waters, rivers, seas, oceans; its atmosphere, its stratosphere, and here and there, earthquakes, volcanic eruptions, tornados, tidal waves.

Although it is a planet dependent on the Sun, this Earth-World is finite, isolated, autonomous, drawing its autonomy from its very dependence. It is a planet that has become peculiar and unique among the other planets of the solar system and the stars of the galaxy. In the midst of this peculiar uniqueness, it has given rise to something unique and peculiar in the whole solar system, if not the galaxy: life

A LIVING EARTH

On the small planet of a small sun at the Milky Way's periphery—a lost galaxy cast adrift among many millions of others—there came about, perhaps 3.8 billion years ago, with birthpangs stirred by eruptions and storms, the first manifestations of life.

The rise of life in a physical world remained incomprehensible as long as living matter was thought to have another nature and enjoy other properties than physicochemical matter and to defy the second principle of thermodynamics that dooms all physical things to entropy, that is, to dispersion and/or disorganization. From 1950 on, following the discovery by Watson and Crick of the genetic code inscribed in the DNA of living cells, it has become clear that life is constituted by the same physicochemical components as the rest of earthly nature, and that it differs from them mainly because of the original complexity of its organization. A few years later, in the early 1970s, Prigogine's thermodynamics showed that certain unstable conditions not only foster disorders and turbulences but also organizing forms that generate and regenerate themselves. It then became conceivable that life emerged from the Earth's disorders and turbulences.

Thus, at the close of this century, it is admissible that living organisms have resulted from nonlinear, organizational complexity issuing from macromolecular chance encounters,[4] perhaps at times at the surface of stones,[5] but finally in whirling liquid environments. The origin of life remains a mystery about which scenarios are ceaselessly elaborated (see Eigen, 1972).[6] But life could only issue from a mix of chance and necessity, in proportions we cannot determine. Physicochemical complexity is a "continuum;" but this continuum allows for many leaps: one separating inner from outer environments, another dealing with energy transfers and the differentiation of these transfers, and, finally, the radical hypercomplexifying leap from a strictly chemical organization to an auto-eco-reorganization equipped with a cognitive dimension (computational-informational-communicational; see Morin, 1985) capable of self-organization, self-reparation, self-reproduction, and the ability to draw organization, energy, and information from its environment.

---

[4]Some of these molecules could have come from meteorites.

[5]Antoine Danchin (1990) has developed the hypothesis, well befitting his way of thinking, that life originated from stones.

[6]To which we must add the scenario of life's extraterrestrial origin, proposed by Crick.

The problem thus becomes: How could such an organization arise on Earth? Is the appearance of life a singular event resulting from a highly improbable accumulation of accidents, or rather the fruit of an evolutionary process that, if not necessary, is at least highly probable?

In favor of probability the following facts offer support:

- The spontaneous formation of macromolecules fit to live in given conditions that we can simulate in laboratories
- The discovery in meteorites of amino-acids that are forerunners to those of life
- Prigogine's thermodynamics, which shows that, in given conditions of instability, organizations are spontaneously constituted; hence, the probability of more and more complex macromolecular combinations in appropriate thermodynamic conditions (vortices)
- The possibility that, in these conditions of encounter and over a long period, a selective process took place on behalf of complementary molecular RNA/protein combinations, capable now of self-replication and of metabolism
- The very high probability that, in a universe of billions upon billions of stars, there exist millions of planets analogous to the Earth and consequently the probable existence of living beings in other regions of the cosmos.

In favor of improbability are the following points:

- The qualitative/quantitative leap (the smallest bacterium is a congeries of many millions of molecules) and the radical discontinuity between the most complex macro-molecular organizations and living auto-eco-reorganization (which is, to repeat, computational-informational-communicational by nature) make the aforesaid highly improbable
- Living organization is in itself highly improbable, in the sense that, following the second principle of thermodynamics, it is the dispersion of life's molecular components that conforms to physical probability, a probability that inevitably leads to death
- Many clues point to the idea that life might have been born only once, which means all living beings would have one and the same ancestor, and which strengthens the hypothesis that a highly improbable chance event would have created it

- There is no sign, no trace of life in the solar system, no message coming to us from the cosmos
- Besides, the proof based on other planets having enjoyed conditions analogous to ours has no validity if, on this very Earth, life has resulted from unparalleled phenomena.

A third hypothesis is worth mentioning: There may exist in the universe very complex organizations, endowed with properties of autonomy, intelligence, even thought, although not based on a nucleo-proteined organization and that would be (now? forever?) impervious to our perception and our intellect.

In any case, we are still in a state of deep uncertainty as to whether life arose inevitably or by chance, necessarily or miraculously, and this uncertainty impacts obviously on the meaning of human lives.

We do, however, know that life emerged both as an emanation and a creation of the Earth.

We know that, even if, as Crick would have it, life's seeds (archeobacteria) were extraterrestrial originally, the Earth is the cradle of life.

We know that earthly life is solitary within the solar system and the Milky Way.

We know that there was apparently one first living being that reproduced, multiplied, and transformed itself into innumerable forms and populated the Earth.

Archeobacteria, then bacteria, proliferated in the air and in the ground, constituting during 2 billion years the only biosphere in which all members communicated by degrees (notably through DNA being injected by one bacterium to another). In the midst of this tellurian solidarity, symbiotic events took place, bringing about the formation of cells with a nucleus, of eubacteria, and of eukaryotes, which came together and organized so as to form polycellular beings, plants, and animals.

It is possible that unicellular algae used solar energy (photosynthesis). In any case, plant life unfolded and gave off oxygen to the atmosphere, making possible aerobic life and the unfolding of the animal world which, deprived of photosynthetic power, sought its energy by consuming other lives.

Life spread over the seas, climbed onto the land, taking shape and covering it with trees and plants, then flew into the air with insects and birds.

Begun some 450 million years ago, the great diversification allows for a multiform, dialogical interaction between animals and plants, in which living beings feed on each other and constitute, through actions at once antagonistic, competitive, and complementary, eco-organizations and ecosystems (see Morin, 1985).

Life's history endures the transformations and cataclysms of the Earth's crust. Its unfolding is inseparable from the formation of seas and continents, from the erecting and eroding of reliefs. Every now and then, minimal modifications of geography, weather, environment, and the genetic code have chain repercussions on the whole. Ecosystems evolve through disorganization and reorganization. Eras follow one another according to a dialectic of innovations, accidents, and catastrophes. Once flowers had sprung into being, an extraordinary cooperation was woven between insects and flowers. It is perhaps a tellurian cataclysm that allowed for the amazing development of mammals benefitting from the massive destruction of dinosaurs, at the end of the secondary era, after a meteorite had crashed to Earth, dug a chasm, and raised such a cloud that a general impoverishment of plants caused the death of the gigantic herbivores.

Forking and branching off, life has displayed throughout 500 million years an utmost diversity: plants, invertebrates, and vertebrates; among these vertebrates, agnathes, fishes, reptiles, mammals; among these mammals—the primates that, over the last 70 million years, spread all over the Ancient and New World (at that time joined together), and, 35 million years ago, the upper primates in Africa and Arabia. From among these primates, some 17 million years ago, humanity's predecessors arose.

In this way, a "tree of life" has taken shape and grown on Earth; this tree obviously does not have a regular trunk and symmetrical branches. It sprouts umbels, clusters, and strobils in all hues and fragrances, a knotwork of boughs in which branches and roots both join and diverge.

The tree of life is also a sphere of life. This sphere, in interaction with geoclimatic conditions, has created many niches that together constitute the biosphere.

Homo, the last and deviating branch on the tree of life, arose inside the biosphere. The latter, joining ecosystems with ecosystems, already covers the whole planet. It is a very thin layer of life and atmosphere as compared to cosmic distances. In the same way the physical earth had been its placenta, so it is with humanity's placenta.

So life, born from the Earth, has entered into partnership with the Earth. Life is the partner of life. Each and every animal life needs bacteria, plants, and other animals. The discovery of ecological partnership is a great and recent discovery. No living being, even human, can break away from the biosphere.

HUMAN IDENTITY

From the moment mythic tales concerning the birth of humanity became problematic, humanity questioned itself about its origin and its nature.

Modern thinkers have turned humans into almost supernatural beings, gradually filling the space vacated by God. Although Bacon, Descartes, Buffon, and Marx assigned humanity the mission of mastering nature and ruling the universe, following Rousseau, romanticism emphasized humanity's umbilical attachment to nature. In this way, among writers and poets, Earth acquired motherly features. Conversely, among technicians and scientists, Earth has been seen as a thing, as an array of objects to be manipulated mercilessly.

Enlightenment rationalism tended to see the same human being, with the same qualities and basic passions, across diverse civilizations, but romanticism, following Herder, underlined the oddities imprinted by cultures into each individual. In this manner, both the unity and diversity of humankind was perceived, although in an either-or fashion and not simultaneously.

During the 19th century, the natural sciences admitted more and more clearly the biological nature of humanity, whereas the human sciences recognized more and more clearly its psychic and cultural aspects. However, the compartmentalization between the sciences, and the oppositions between schools of thought, made it impossible to include these three features into one multisided conception, and each of these points of view, hypostatizing the feature perceived, screened off the others.

In other respects, the biological recognition of human unity would not by itself attenuate the hierarchical ordering of the species into higher and lower races. Even though, influenced by the Enlightenment, western humanism granted equal rights to each human being, western ethnocentrism denied "primitive" and "backward" people the status of fully mature and reasonable human beings.

During the 19th century as well, the birth of humankind was ascribed to biological evolution and no longer to a creator God. It was admitted that humans descended from monkeys, but it was equally contended that, upon leaving the tree of their ancestors, humans abandoned it forever, maintaining with the primates a merely anatomical and physiological kinship. Up to 1960, then, *homo sapiens* arose suddenly, with its intelligence, tools, language, and culture, similar to Minerva issuing from the head of an invisible Jupiter.

Humanity's insularity became questionable during the 1960s. The observations of Janet Van Lawick-Goodall (1971), then the "talks" of the Gardners and of Premack with chimpanzees (Morin & Piattelli-Palmarini, 1974), brought us mentally closer to our former ancestors, who had now become our cousins. Although these findings drew primates and humans closer together, the discoveries of Louis and Mary Leakey (1959) in the caves of the Olduwai, of their son Richard (1972) at Lake Rudolph, and of Yves Coppens (1974) in the Omo Valley revealed biped hominids, a few million years old, having a 600-cubic-centimeter brain already capable of fabricating tools, weapons, and shelters. *Homo sapiens* did not arise, then, armed from head to toe, some 50,000 years ago, but emerged in the course of a multimillion years process of hominization. These hominids, no longer extant, were already human. We are the latest human beings, distinguished by a brain of some 1,500 cubic centimeters.

As life stemmed from the Earth, thanks to a unique local situation, so humanity stemmed from life, thanks to a unique animal species—the tree-dwelling primates of the African tropical forest, to which these primates belong and which, at the same time, they have outgrown. It is owing to new and peculiar conditions in the history of the Earth that a climatic change, bringing about in southern Africa a regression of the tropical forest and a progression of the savannah, pushed our ancestors, already in the process of becoming hominids, to develop bipedalism—running, hunting, and the systematic use of tools. Such is the beginning of the very long adventure of hominization, which continued with the domestication of fire by *Homo erectus*. The process accelerated during the last 500,000 years. Tools became ever more efficient, hunting techniques developed, shelters built, and garments made. Interpersonal relations became more complicated, affective ties embellished by friendship and love between men/women, parents/children, and, within this multidimensional process, hominids underwent an anatomical, cerebral, psychological, affective, and social transformation: The dawn of language, probably before Homo sapiens itself, operated the crucial cultural change[7] to humanity.

---

[7]Culture is a body of rules, knowledge, techniques, learning, values, and myths, which allows for and insures the high complexity of human

Homo, however, did not escape from its animality during this transformation. *Homo* is not a postprimate but a superprimate, who has improved on abilities already present in the higher primates, although these were spread thin, transient, and occasional, such as the making of tools, hunting, and walking with the lower limbs. *Homo* is not a postmammal but a supermammal, who has inwardly developed the affective warmth of mother-child, brother-sister relationships, has preserved it as an adult, and extended it to loving and friendly relationships. *Homo*, not a supervertebrate, but an average one, does not know how to fly, how to swim in deep water, and, as far as running is concerned, lags far behind tigers, horses or gazelles, except that it has, in the end, outstripped the vertebrates and their performances through creating techniques that endow it with speed on the ground, navigation on and under water, and transportation in the air. *Homo* is a living being, considering that the many billion self-renewing cells of which each individual is constituted are all daughters-sisters of the first living being, whose sisterly offspring has produced, via symbiosis, the eukaryote cells of the plant and animal worlds. These daughter-sister cells are also mothers of the cells they produce by dividing into two. Finally, *Homo* is a super-being because it has accomplished in a superior fashion very many capabilities of living organization.

Its biological identity is completely earthly because, on Earth, life arose out of earthly chemical mixtures in the midst of whirling waters and under stormy clouds. This physicochemical earthly identity, inherent in all living organizations, enfolds a cosmic polyidentity because the carbon atoms necessary to earthly life were formed within the furious forge of suns antedating our own, and because the billions upon billions of particles that make up our bodies were born 15 billion years ago at the radiant dawn of our universe.

The mythologies of other civilizations rooted the human world in nature; not so, *Homo occidentalis,* who, up to the mid-19th century, was totally ignorant and unconscious of its earthly and cosmic identity. Contemporary philosophy and anthropology continue to inhibit any awareness of, and any inference from, humanity's animal and living identity, seeing as irrational "vitalism" or perverse "biologism" any acknowledgement of our earthly physical and biological rootedness.

---

individuals and societies, and which, because it is not innate, needs to be transmitted and taught to each individual during his or her learning stage in order to perpetuate itself and maintain humanity's high anthropological complexity.

Homo the super-living has created new spheres of life: the sphere of the spirit, the sphere of myths, the sphere of ideas, and the sphere of consciousness. In the process of producing these new forms of life—forms that depend on language, concepts, and ideas, and that feed the mind and consciousness—we gradually became estranged from the living animal world, hence, the twofold status of *homo*. On the one hand, we belong completely to biological, physical, and cosmic nature. On the other hand, we belong completely to culture, that is, to the universe of speech, myth, ideas, reason, and consciousness.

Starting from and reaching beyond its identities that root it to the Earth and bespeak its place in the Cosmos, *Homo* also produces its typically human identities in connection with the family, ethnic group, culture, religion, society, and nation.

ANTHROPOLOGICAL UNITY

However diverse its appurtenances in terms of genes, lands, communities, rituals, myths, and ideas, *Homo sapiens* has a fundamental identity shared by all its representatives. Whether issued or not from a unique ancestor, it depends on a specific genetic sameness that allows for the interfecundation between all men and women, whatever their race. This genetic sameness extends into morphological, anatomical, and physiological sameness. The cerebral sameness of *Homo sapiens* is shown in the peculiar organization of the human brain as compared to other primates. There is finally a psychological and affective sameness. Of course, laughter, tears, and smiles are diversely modulated, inhibited, or exhibited according to cultures, but notwithstanding the extreme diversity of these cultures and of the prevailing personality types, laughters, tears, and smiles are universal, and their inborn quality is revealed among people born deaf, mute, and blind, people who smile, cry, and laugh without having been able to imitate anyone (Eibl-Eibesfeldt, 1971, 1972, 1974).

The diaspora of *Homo sapiens* began 1,300 centuries ago, covered Africa and Eurasia, crossed the Bering strait—at that time dried up—100,000 years ago, reached Australia and New Guinea 40,000 years ago, and finally populated the islands of Polynesia a few thousand years before the current era.

In spite of this diaspora, and in spite of physical differentiations in cultures, and the fact that languages became mutually unintelligible, rituals and customs incomprehensible, and peculiar beliefs unyielding to one another, everywhere there has been myth; rationality, strategy, and invention; dance, rhythm, and music. Everywhere there has been—unevenly expressed or repressed according to cultures—pleasure, love, affection, friendship, anger, and hatred. Everywhere there has been proliferating imagination, and, however different their recipes and their proportions, always and everywhere there has been an inseparable mixture of clear-headedness and folly.

Every sexed species brings forth individuals who are different due not only to the almost limitless combinations between two hereditary patrimonies, but also to the utmost diversity of conditions, food, influences, and hazards bearing on the embryo's formation as well as on that of the newborn. The more complex the species, the greater also are individual differences. As far as humans are concerned, diversification grows, multiplies, and intensifies with the events and accidents of childhood and adolescence, with the conformity or resistance to family, culture, and societal influences. Since the archaic institution of exogamy and the prohibition of incest, culture stimulates and increases the gene pool. Wars and invasions have also enlarged the pool through rapes, abductions, enslavement, and the mixing of populations. Furthermore, traveling, coupling, and marrying also bring genetic diversity to individuals of the same ethnic group.

Diversification is also psychocultural. Depending on the culture, there are predominant types of attitudes, behaviors, aggressiveness, good temper, and so on. In every civilization, and particularly in our own, each individual assumes different personalities, according to his or her mood and according to the person he or she meets, confronts, or tolerates (e.g., child, relative, wife, mistress, boss, underling, a rich person or beggar, etc.). Two radically opposed personalities—anger and love—appear within each individual. Each individual commands an array of multiple personalities that are susceptible to being activated. This multiplicity, diversity, and complexity *also* contributes to the sameness of our species.

Every human being is a cosmos; every individual swarms with virtual personalities; every psyche exudes a multitude of fantasies, dreams, and ideas. Everyone experiences, from birth to death, an unfathomable tragedy, marked by cries of pain, orgasms, laughter, tears, prostration, greatness, and misery. Everyone harbors treasures, deficiencies, faults, and chasms. Everyone harbors the possibility of love and self-sacrifice, of hatred and resentment, of revenge and forgiveness. To acknowledge this is once again to acknowledge human unity. The principle of identity applied to humans is that of *unitas multiplex*—multifaceted oneness, whether biologically, culturally, or individually conceived.

Such is the great theme of the world's poetry and literature. However much separated by language, time, or culture, we can communicate with strangers via literature, poetry, music, and cinema. We can recognize this common identity—albeit variously expressed—in the Albanian fugitive, the Sardinian shepherd, the Samurai, the Parisian wretch, the St. Petersburg culprit, or the innocent.

The differences caused by the diversity of language, myths, and ethnocentric cultures have concealed our common bioanthropological identity. In the eyes of archaic people, the stranger is a god or a demon. In historic times, the enemy is killed or, by being turned into a slave, becomes an animated tool. The protective enclosures of each self-centered culture during humanity's diaspora have henceforth, in our Planetary Era, undesirable consequences. Most fragments of humanity in current communication have become disquieting and hostile to one another as a result of this very communication: Differences hitherto ignored have become oddities, madness, or ungodliness, sources of misunderstanding and conflicts. Societies see themselves as competing species and set about killing one another. Monotheist religions wipe out polytheist gods, and each sovereign divinity fights against its competitor by way of sending its faithful to death and murder. Nationhood and ideology have constructed new barriers, stirred up new hatreds. The islamicist, the capitalist, the communist, the fascist have lost sight of their humanity; *hence, the all-important necessity of unmasking, revealing, in and through its diversity, the unity of the species, human identity, and the anthropological universals.*

We can recover and accomplish the unity of humankind. The latter, lost in and through the diaspora of *Homo sapiens* among continents and islands, was denied more than recognized during the Planetary Era. We must recover it, not by a bulldozing homogenization of cultures, but rather by a full recognition and a full flowering of cultural diversity that would not prevent processes of unification and diversification from operating on broader levels.

Thus, nation building has integrated and attenuated, without thereby dissolving, the diversity of provincial ethnicities or ethnic groups and has brought about participation in a broader national unity, itself the origin of new diversities between national cultures. Similarly, the metanational stage should in no way melt national peculiarities, but should take away from the State its absolute sovereignty and foster ethnic and cultural mixings, notably in big cities, that breed a new unity as well as new diversities.

To recover or accomplish the unity of humankind would mean first of all to concretize, for all to see, the common identity. This is what empathic mental flashes bring about when we see on television hunger-stricken Somali children or women and children shelled at Sarajevo. What happens is obviously a correlated heightening of heartfelt compassion, spiritual humanism, a true universalism, and a respect for difference, which will lead us to overcome the ego-ethno-centric and ideological blindness that makes us see the stranger as but a stranger, and that makes us see those who threaten us, whether truly or falsely, as monsters or sordid beings. However, as I contend later, a reform of the mind and a moral reform would be required so that each and everyone recognize in each and everyone else a human identity.

The identity of humanity, that is, its complex unity and diversity, has been cloaked and betrayed, in the midst of the Planetary Era, by the specialized and compartmentalized unfolding of the sciences. The biological characteristics of humanity have been apportioned to departments of biology and to medical teaching. The psychological, cultural, and social characteristics have been parceled out and set in the various departments of human and social sciences, in such a way that sociology has been unable to see society, that history has kept to itself, and that economics has extracted from *Homo sapiens demens* the bloodless residue of *Homo economicus*. Worse still, the idea of humanity has been broken into dislocated fragments, and a triumphant structuralism has fancied itself capable of removing definitively this ridiculous fantasy. Philosophy, locked away in its abstractions, has only been able to rejoin humanity through the experiences and existential tensions of the likes of Pascal, Kierkegaard, and Heidegger, without ever succeeding in linking subjective experience to anthropological knowledge.

It is no accident that anthropological knowledge has not been reconstituted. The compartmentalization of disciplines and the sclerosis of universities have prevented its reconstitution, all the more so because the data that would have allowed the connections to be made had not yet been discovered. Almost simultaneously, during the years 1955-1960, one sees the emergence of the first theories of self-organization (Foerster & Zopf, 1962), complexity (Bronowski, 1969; von Neumann 1966), and the first attempts at a universal dialectics of order, disorder, and organization. From this point forward, on the basis of the idea of auto-eco-organization and of the integration of disorder in cerebral/mental organization, as well as on the basis of the advances in neuroscience, we can begin to understand the fabulous machine that is the brain of *Homo sapiens demens*, with its hundred billion neurons and many trillion synaptic connections. It is at last possible, since 1970, to start building a fundamental anthropology (Morin, 1979).

Anthropology, as a multidimensional discipline (joining within itself the biological, sociological, economical, historical, and psychological) seeking to disclose the complex unity and diversity of humanity, will rise in truth only in correlation with the reconstitution of the aforesaid disciplines, until now separate and compartmentalized. This reconstitution will involve the transition from reductive, mutilating, isolating, cataloguing, and abstracting thought to the principles of complex thinking (see Chapter 8).

EARTH AWARENESS

The revolution that took place in the 15th century with regard to how we picture the world, the Earth, and humanity was no more than a small cabinet crisis as compared to the awesome upheavals brought about by the scientific findings of the late 20th century.

We have been obliged to forsake an orderly, perfect, and eternal universe in favor of a moving and expanding universe, born in radiation, in which order, disorder, and organization enter into dialogue in a manner at once complementary, concurrent, and antagonistic. We have been obliged to forsake the notion of specific living substance, quickened by a breath all its own, so as to discover the complexity of living organization as it emerges out of earthly physicochemical processes. We have been obliged to forsake the notion of a supernatural human being belonging to a separate creation and rather have allowed our being to emerge from a process wherein it breaks away from nature without, however, dissociating from it.

It is because we have rightly examined the sky that we can take root on the Earth. It is because we have rightly examined the Earth that we can root life in it. It is because we have rightly examined life that we can take root in it.

The Earth is not the sum of an addition: a physical planet, plus the biosphere, plus humankind. The Earth is a physical/biological/anthropological complex totality, in which life emerges from the Earth's history and humankind from earthly life's history.

Life is a biophysical organizing force at work in the atmosphere it has created, on the ground, underground, and in the seas, where it has expanded and has grown.

Humanity is a planetary and biospheric entity.

We are many millions of light years removed from a human-centered cosmos, and yet we can no more look at humanity, nature, life, and the cosmos as so many neatly separated entities, impervious to one another.

Our closing 5th century of the Planetary Era lays bare the facts of our destiny thus far unknown:

- We are lost in the cosmos
- Life is alone in the solar system and possibly in the galaxy
- Earth, life, humanity, and consciousness are the outcome of a peculiar adventure, whose progress has been marked by amazing fits and starts
- Humanity is a member of the community of life, even though human consciousness stands alone;
- Humanity's common destiny, which is typical of the Planetary Era, is inseparable from the common destiny of the Earth.

This new knowledge, which enlightens us about our earthly destiny, leads us to a new ignorance. A part of this ignorance will be lifted, but another, which owes to the limitations of the human mind (Morin 1992), will remain forever. Similarly, new certainties lead us to a new uncertainty. We know now where we come from, but we do not know what we come from, that, is we are uncertain as to the origin of the world and the origin of life. We do not know why there is a world rather than nothing, and we do not know where this world is going. We exist in a universe neither trivial, normal, nor obvious.

The Earth is a small cosmic garbage can that has become, against all odds, not only a very complex planet but also a garden— our garden. The life it has produced, which it enjoys, which we enjoy, does not flow from any a priori necessity. It is possibly unique in the cosmos; it is alone in the solar system; it is fragile, rare, precious, because rare and fragile.

We have learned that all that exists has come into being within chaos and turbulence and must hold out against huge destructive forces. The cosmos has organized itself through disintegration. The sun beams at the temperature of its explosion. Perhaps humans would not have developed had we not had to rise to so many deadly challenges, from the advance of the savannah over the tropical forests to the glaciation of temperate regions. The adventure of hominization took place in want and pain. Homo is the child of *Paros* and *Penia*. All that lives must regenerate itself incessantly: the sun, the biosphere, society, culture, and love. It often means misfortune for us as well as grace and privilege. All that is precious on Earth is fragile and rare. So it is, too, for our consciousness.

Here we are, then, tiny humans on the tiny film of life surrounding the tiny planet lost in the gigantic universe (which perhaps is itself tiny in a proliferating pluriverse[8]). Notwithstanding, this planet is a world, a universe swarming with billions upon billions of individuals, with each human being a cosmos of dreams, yearnings, and desires.

Our earthly genealogical tree and our earthly identity card are today finally knowable at the end of the 5th century of the Planetary Era. It is precisely today—just when the societies scattered throughout the globe are communicating, just when the destiny of humanity has become a collective concern—that they begin to make sense and help us recognize our Homeland Earth.

---

[8]On the notion of many worlds, see Morin (1981).

3

The Earth in Crisis

Throughout the 20th Century, the economy, population, development, and ecology have become problems that concern all nations and civilizations, that is, the planet as a whole.

Some of these problems are currently receiving much attention. I review them briefly before turning to other, sometimes less obvious ones that I consider "of the second order," the tangle among all of which constitutes the problem of problems.

PROBLEMS OF THE FIRST ORDER

Global Economic Disorder

The global market can be seen as a self-organizing system that produces its own regulations, despite the evident and inevitable disorder in which it operates. One can suppose that, by means of a few international authorities, it could dampen its booms, reabsorb its depressions, and, sooner or later, seal off and inhibit its crises.

All self-organizing systems, however, are in fact auto-eco-organizing systems, that is, they are autonomous/dependent with regard to their eco-systems. One cannot consider the economy as an enclosed entity. The economic sphere is autonomous/dependent relative to other spheres (sociological, cultural, political), which themselves are autonomous/dependent relative to one another. Thus, the market economy implies a coherent set of institutions, but this coherent set is lacking at the planetary scale.

It is the relation to the noneconomic that is missing in the science of economics. The latter is a science whose mathematization and formalization are increasingly rigorous and sophisticated, but these qualities involve the failings of an abstraction that cuts itself off from its social, cultural, and political context. It gains its formal precision by forgetting about the complexity of the real situation, that is, by forgetting that the economy depends on that which depends on it. Moreover, economistic knowledge, which encloses itself in the economic sphere, is incapable of anticipating perturbations and becoming, and is thus blind to the economic itself.

The global economy seems to oscillate between crisis and noncrisis, misarrangements and rearrangements. Profoundly deregulated, it ceaselessly reestablishes partial regulations, often at the price of destructions (of surpluses, for example, to maintain the monetary value of products) and a chain reaction of human, cultural, moral, and social havoc (unemployment, increase in the cultivation of drug-bearing plants). Economic growth has, since the 19th century, been not only the engine but also the regulator of the economy by increasing demand at the same time as supply. However, this growth has, at the same time, irremediably destroyed rural civilizations and traditional cultures. It has brought considerable improvements in the standard of living, but it has simultaneously brought about perturbations in the way people live.

In any case, the global market is now deeply fraught with:

- Disorder in the trade of raw materials, with its series of disastrous consequences
- The artificial and precarious character of monetary regulations (the intervention of central banks to regulate exchange rates, to prevent, for example, the drop of the dollar)
- The inability to find economic regulations for monetary problems (external debts, including the enormous debt of developing countries, totaling some 100 billion dollars) and monetary regulations for economic problems (to allow or restore freedom in the pricing of bread, cous-cous, etc.) that are at the same time social and political problems

- The gangrene of the mafias, which is spreading throughout the world
- Fragility in the face of para-economic perturbations (the closing of borders, blockades, wars)
- Competition in the global market, which entails the specialization of local or national economies, and which brings about increasingly vital solidarities between each and everyone; however, by the same token, in the event of crises or social and political upheavals, the destruction of these solidarities becomes fatal for each and everyone.

Moreover, economic growth causes new disorders. Its exponential character not only creates a multiform process of degradation of the biosphere, but equally a multiform process of degradation of the psychosphere, that is, of our mental, affective, and moral lives. All this entails a series and cycle of consequences.

The effect on civilization produced by the commodification of everything, well foretold by Marx—after water, the seas and sunlight, human organs, blood, sperm, eggs, and fetal tissue become merchandise—is the disappearance of the gift freely given, of service rendered, and the near disappearance of the nonmonetary, which entails the erosion of values other than the lure of gain, financial interest, or the thirst for riches.

Finally, an infernal machine has been set in motion; as René Passet (1992) put it: "A senseless international competition imposes the search, at any price, for surplus productivity which, instead of being spread out among consumers, workers, and investors, is essentially devoted to the reduction of costs for new surplus productivity, which itself is etc." In this competition, technological developments are immediately used for productivity and profit, creating increased unemployment[1] and disturbing human rhythms.

To be sure, competition remains at once the great stimulator and regulator of the economy, and its disturbances, as in the formation of monopolies, can be combatted through antitrust laws. However, what is new is that international competition already nourishes an acceleration to which conviviality and possibilities for reform are sacrificed, and which, if there is no deceleration, is leading us to explosion, disintegration, or maybe mutation.

---

[1]The automobile assembly line allowed for the creation of jobs for mechanics, used car salesmen, and so on. This is not the case with computerized technology.

Global Demographic Disorder

There were one billion human beings in 1800. There are six billion today. Ten billion are predicted by the year 2050.

Progress in hygiene and medicine in poorer countries are lowering infant mortality without lowering the birth rate. Well-being and transformations in civilized life, with which it is associated, diminish the birth rate in richer countries. The increase of the poor world, which is more populated than the rich world, outstrips the decrease of the latter. But for how long? Catastrophic forecasts point to the surpassing of the possibilities of subsistence, the generalization of famines, and the migratory spread West of the wretched. Yet there are factors that can slow things down, such as antibirth policies (India, China) and the trend toward the reduction of offspring accompanying progress in well-being and the modernization of social values.

Thus, one must not isolate the demographic process but contextualize it within the totality of social, cultural, and political processes.

Demographic evolution brings, as ever, its own uncertainty. To date, Europe has not anticipated the great modifications in the rise and fall of its populations. An unexpected population surge began during 1940 and continued after the war, then a brutal falling off began in Berlin toward the end of the 1950s and became generalized throughout most of Europe. There has been no guarantee that current global population growth will necessarily continue in an exponential fashion.

The Ecological Crisis

The metanational and planetary character of the ecological peril appeared with the announcement of the death of the oceans by Ehrlich in 1969 and with the Meadows report commissioned by the Club of Rome in 1972.

Following the global apocalyptic prophecies of 1969-1972, there was a period of increase in local ecological degradations of fields, woods, lakes, rivers, and polluted urban agglomerations. It was only during the 1980s that the following catastrophes arose. First, there were the great local catastrophes that had widespread consequences, for example, Seveso, Bhopal, Three Mile Island, Chernobyl, the drying of the Aral sea, the pollution of Lake Baïkal, and cities on the verge of asphyxiation (Mexico, Athens). The ecological menace ignores national boundaries: The pollution of the Rhine concerns Switzerland, France, Germany, the Netherlands, and the North Sea. The fallout from Chernobyl reached beyond the European continent.

Second, more general problems have occurred in industrialized countries, such as the contamination of water, including ground water, the poisoning of the soil from excess pesticides and fertilizers, massive urbanization of fragile ecological regions (such as coastal zones), acid rain, and the stockpiling of toxic waste. Nonindustrialized countries have witnessed desertification, deforestation, soil erosion and salinization, floods, the runaway urbanization of megapolises poisoned by sulphur dioxide (which causes asthma), carbon monoxide (which leads to cerebral and cardiac trouble), and nitrous dioxide (an immunodepressant).

Furthermore, global problems have involved the planet as a whole: CO_2 emissions that intensify the green-house effect, poisoning micro-organisms that recycle waste, and altering important vital cycles; and the deterioration of the stratospheric ozone, the ozone hole in Antarctica, and excess ozone in the troposphere (the lowest layer of the atmosphere).

The ecological consciousness/conscience is evidence of our awakening to the global problem and global peril that threaten the planet. In the words of Jean-Marie Pelt: "Humans are destroying, one by one, the systems of defense of the planetary organism."

Reactions to the threat were, to begin with, mostly local and technical. Then ecological associations and parties multiplied and ministries of the environment were created in 70 countries. The Stockholm conference of 1972 gave rise to international organizations devoted to the environment (PNUE) and international research and action programs were established (the United Nations program on the environment, the UNESCO program on Man and Biosphere). Finally, the Rio conference brought together 175 States in 1992. The main question is one of conciliating the necessity for ecological protection with the necessity for Third World economic development. The idea of "sustainable development" implies a dialogical encounter of the idea of development, which involves an increase in pollution, with the idea of the environment, which requires the limiting of pollution:

The idea of development, however, remains tragically underdeveloped (as discussed later). It has not yet been truly rethought, not even with the concept of "sustainable development."

The Rio conference adopted a declaration on forests, and an agreement on the climate and the protection of biodiversity. It established Action Plan 21 (the 21st Century), which aims to unite nations so as to work together to protect the biosphere.

It is only a beginning. The biosphere is continuing to deteriorate. Tropical deforestation is accelerating; biological diversity is diminishing. Degradation continues to outstrip regradation.

There are two main scenarios for the next 30 years. The "pessimists" see an irreversible race toward the generalized degradation of the biosphere, with a modification of the climates, a rise in temperature and evaporation/transpiration, a rise in sea levels (30 to 140 centimeters), and an extension of arid zones, all with a probable population of 10 billion human beings. The "optimists" think that the biosphere possesses the potential for autoregeneration and immunological defense, which would allow it to protect itself, and that the population will stabilize at around 8.5 billion human beings.

In any event, we must proceed with caution. What we need is an ecologized thinking, a thinking that, founded on the concept of auto-eco-organization, considers the vital link of every living, human, or social system to its environment.

The Crisis of Development

The idea of development was key in the years after the war. There was a so-called developed world divided in two: one "capitalist," the other "socialist." Each brought their own model of development to the Third World. At present, after the multiple miscarriages of the Western, "capitalist" model of development, the crisis of state communism has led to the failure of the "socialist" model as well. What is more, there exists a global crisis of development. *The problem of development runs headlong into the cultural/civilizational problem along with the economic problem.* The very word *development,* by its own definition, includes within itself and stimulates underdevelopment. It must henceforth be problematized; but to effect this problematization, we must first consider the second type of problem.

PROBLEMS OF THE SECOND ORDER

The Dual Process, both Antagonistic and Linked, of the Solidarization and Balkanization of the Planet

The 17th and 18th centuries witnessed the self-assertion of the first European and North American nation-states. The 19th century witnessed the expansion of the nation-state throughout Europe and

South America. The 20th century generalized the formula for the nation-state both in Europe (with the dislocation of the Ottoman, Austro-Hungarian, and Soviet empires) and the rest of the world (with the death of the British, French, Dutch, and Portuguese colonial empires). The U.N. currently includes some 200 sovereign States.

The first nation-states (France, England, Spain) brought together and integrated diverse ethnic groups within a broader cultural space, where a national identity was gradually forged. The polyethnic states formed during the 20th century did not have the historical time required for national integration, and they disintegrated with the lifting of the coercion that maintained their unity, as has been demonstrated in Yugoslavia. Many nation-states were formed on the basis of claims to sovereignty on the part of ethnic groups freeing themselves from an empire. Many of these groups, after centuries of intermingling, themselves have minorities in their midst. Out of this situation arise numberless conflicts and nationalist exasperations, sometimes explosive, at other times mastered under pressure from the great powers.

Increasingly, throughout this century, one sees the assertion of the irresistible aspiration to constitute a nation equipped with a state, where before there was but an ethnic group. This aspiration often expresses itself in opposition to economic realities and interests, which shows that the demand for nationhood has other sources (the need for autonomy and self-affirmation, the need for regeneration and community).

It is absolutely remarkable that now, as a rule, ethnic and religious regeneration or rerooting crystallizes around the nation-state. To comprehend this phenomenon, one must understand that the nation-state harbors an extremely "hot" mythological/affective element. The terms *mother country* or *fatherland* (*patrie*[2]) evoke the qualities of the maternal and the paternal. These matripatriotic qualities give maternal value to the mother country, to the land as mother, whom one naturally loves, and they attribute paternal strength to the state to which one owes unconditional obedience. Sharing a native land creates a fraternal community among its "children."[3] This mythological fraternity can bring together millions of individuals who share no ties of blood. In this way the nation restores, in modern guise, the warmth of family, clannish or tribal

[2]The French word *patrie* is feminine in gender, but masculine in its etymology *(pater* = father).

[3]*"Enfants de la patrie"* in the French text, quoting *La Marseillaise*, ("Children of the Nation"), France's national anthem.

ties, themselves lost to modern civilization, which, for its part, tends to atomize individuals. The nation restores to the adult its infantile sense of being safe and at home. At the same time, the State brings force, arms, authority, and defense. Henceforth, disoriented individuals, faced with the crises of the present and the crises of the future, find in the nation-state the security and the community for which they feel the need.

It is, paradoxically, the Planetary Era itself that has permitted and favored the generalized break-up into nation-states: In fact, the call to nationhood is stimulated by the movement to revitalize ancestral identity, which itself is a reaction against the planetary trend toward cultural homogenization. This call is intensified by the generalized crisis of the future. Along with the revitalization of the familial/mythological past, the nation-state allows for the organization of the present and the confrontation of the future. It is the nation-state that, through technology, administration, and the army, brings greatness and strength to the community. Thus, the nation-state corresponds at once to an archaic need awakened by modern times and to a modern need that reawakens the archaic one.

With the collapse of empires, including the recent collapse of the Soviet empire, the dislocation into nations, even mininations, has been liberating, and ethnic and national revitalization has potential for reform. Yet the polyethnic nation-states, newly emerged from dismantled empires, do not have enough history behind them to integrate their ethnic groups or their minorities, which could consequently become a source for conflicts and wars. These nation-states subjugate, expel, or annihilate what the city or the empire might have tolerated: an ethnic minority.

The absolute character of their sovereignty, their refusal to acknowledge any superior decision-making body; the blind, conflictual, and often paranoid character of the relations between States; the radical insufficiency of an embryonic United Nations, whose authority and supranational status is biased and incomplete, all of this has brought about a situation of generalized balkanization at the very moment the Planetary Era demands the cooperation of nation states and, with respect to the vital questions that concern humanity as a whole, the overcoming of their absolute power. In fact, the proliferation of new nations impedes the formation of vast confederations or federations required by the intensified interdependence of the world's problems. Thus, after having exhausted its historical fertility (which was to establish vaster cultural spaces than those offered by cities and ones better integrated than empires), the absolutely sovereign nation-state imposes itself in a universal fashion, almost everywhere dislocating the potential for association[4] and inhibiting the constitution of cohesive metanational authorities.

In any case, the nation-states, including the great polyethnic nations, are now too small for the great problems, which, henceforth, are inter- and transnational in scope. Economic problems or problems of development, techno-industrial civilization, the homogenization of styles and ways of living, the disintegration of the age-old world of the peasant, or problems with the ecosystem, or with drugs, are all planetary problems that exceed the competence of nations. Moreover, the tendency to isolationism and generalized balkanization must be numbered among the principal threats at this turn of the millennium.

Cutting across antagonism between nations, religious antagonisms are being reactivated, notably in zones of both interference and fracture, such as India/Pakistan and the Middle East. The antagonism of modernity/tradition deteriorates into the antagonism of modernity/fundamentalism. The antagonism of democracy/totalitarianism has diminished, but only to make way for the virulent antagonism of democracy/dictatorship. The East/West antagonism feeds off these antagonisms as it feeds into them, as does the North/South antagonism, to all of which one must add the antagonistic economic and strategic interests of the great powers. All of these antagonisms run together in the globe's great fault lines (including the one that runs from Armenia/Azerbaïdjan to the Sudan) and become concentrated wherever there are mixed religions and ethnic groups, arbitrary boundaries between states, exasperated rivalries, and all types of injustices, as in the Middle East.

Finally, recall the triple crisis that dug a trough from Gdansk to Vladivostok: a political crisis in which the collapse of totalitarianism only made way for uncertain and fragile democratic embryos; an economic crisis into which whole populations plunged, losing the securities and minimum vital requirements of an old system without yet having acquired the hoped-for advantages of a new one; and a national crisis in which ethnic groups with newly gained national sovereignty opposed their own minorities, who claimed the same rights and opposed the nations responsible for these minorities, all of which provoked a critical rise in nationalism. These three crises are mutually supportive: Nationalist hysteria is favored by the economic crisis, and each of these favors the appearance of new dictatorships. As the Israeli philosopher Leibovitz put it: "One passes easily from humanism to nationalism and from nationalism to brutishness."

---

[4]The only counterexample, which has yet to become exemplary, is the community born in the West of Europe.

We are only at the beginning of the formation of this historical cyclone of mutually infectious crises, and no one knows what will finally result in Europe from the meeting of the associative flux originating in the West and the dissociative wave originating in the East.

At the same time, the crisis in Africa[5] goes from bad to worse when, all at once, there is the collapse of "socialist" dictatorships, the inability to replace them with democracies, the withdrawal of Western investments, the weakness or corruption of administrations, and endemic tribal and/or religious wars—all of which translates into devastations and growing famines in Somalia, Ethiopia, the Sudan, and Mozambique.

Neither is the Asian continent immune from the convulsions, which, in the event of ethnic dislocations and wars in China and India, would lead to human cataclysms.

In this way, the 20th century has at the same time both created and torn a unique planetary fabric. Its fragments avoid and bristle at one another, they fight among themselves and tend to destroy the fabric without which they would neither have existed nor developed to this point. States dominate the world scene like so many drunk and brutal Titans, simultaneously powerful and impotent. How can we survive their barbarous reign?

The Universal Crisis of the Future

Europe had spread the faith in progress the world over. Societies, torn from their traditions, no longer enlightened their development by heeding the lessons of the past, but by heading straight for a promising and promised future. Time flowed upward. Progress was marked by the very steps of human history, and it was propelled by developments in science, technology, and reason. The loss of the relation to the past was replaced and compensated for by gains from the march toward the future.

Modern faith in development, progress, and the future had spread all over the world. This faith constituted the common foundation of Western democratic-capitalist ideology, in which progress promised earthly goods and well-being, as well as of the communist ideology with its religion of earthly salvation, that went as far as promising a "socialist paradise."

Progress fell twice into crisis during the first half of this century with the barbarous unleashing of the two World Wars, which

---

[5]In 1960, Africa accounted for 9% of international trade and was nutritionally self-sufficient.

polarized and regressed the most advanced nations. Yet the religion of progress found an antidote that exalted its faith right when it should have collapsed. The horrors of the two wars were looked upon as the reactions of ancient barbarities and even as the apocalyptic heralds of blessed times. To the revolutionaries, these horrors arose from the convulsions of capitalism and imperialism, and they in no way put the promise of progress in question. To the evolutionists, these wars were detours that only delayed for a time the march forward. So when Nazism and Stalinist communism imposed themselves, their barbarous features were masked by their "socialist" promises of prosperity and happiness.

The postwar period (1945) saw the renewal of great progressivist hopes. An excellent future was restored, whether with the idea of the radiant tomorrow promised by communism or with the idea of a more peaceful and prosperous tomorrow promised by the ideals of industrial society. Everywhere in the Third World, the idea of development was supposed to usher in a future liberated from the worst obstacles that weigh on the human condition.

Yet everything was shaken during in the 1970s. The radiant tomorrow was overturned: The socialist revolution revealed its Dantesque face in the U.S.S.R, China, Vietnam, Cambodia, and even Cuba, the latter long considered the pocket-sized "socialist paradise." Then the totalitarian system imploded in the U.S.S.R, and everywhere the faith in the "socialist" future decomposed. In the West, the cultural crisis of 1968 was followed in 1973 by the sinking of Western economies into a lengthy depressionary phase. Finally, in the Third World, the failures of development led to regressions, stagnations, famines, and civil/tribal/religious wars. The beacons of the future had been extinguished. The futurists ceased their pronouncements, and some even closed up shop.[6] The ship of the Earth sailed through night and fog.

During this same period, the very core of the faith in progress—science/technology/industry—was progressively corroded. Science revealed an increasingly radical ambivalence: The mastery of nuclear energy through the physical sciences led not only to human progress but also to human annihilation. The bombs of Hiroshima and Nagasaki, followed by the nuclear arms race of the great and middle powers, weighed heavily on the fate of the planet. Ambivalence penetrated biology in 1980: Developments in genetics

---

[6]As did the Center for Futures Research at the University of Southern California. Surviving institutions are essentially devoted to short-term technological programs, as with the Palo Alto-based Institute for the Future.

and molecular biology led to the first genetic manipulations and herald manipulations of brain chemistry for the control and subjugation of the mind.

Also during this same period, the byproducts of industrial wastes, along with the application of industrial methods to agriculture, the fisheries, and animal husbandry, caused increasingly massive and generalized ill effects and pollution, which threatened the Earth's biosphere and even its psychosphere.

Thus, the developmental triad of science/technology/ industry was everywhere losing its providential character. The idea of modernity was still powerful and full of promise wherever people dreamed of well-being and technological means of liberation. Yet it was beginning to be questioned in the world of well-being already acquired. Modernity had been and still remains a civilizational complex animated by an optimistic dynamism. However, the problematization of the triad that animates this dynamism rendered modernity itself problematic. Modernity harbored the ideas of individual emancipation, the generalized secularization of values, and the distinction between the true, the beautiful, and the good. However, individualism henceforth no longer only meant autonomy and emancipation but also atomization and anonymization. Secularization meant not only liberation from religious dogmas but also loss of foundations, anxiety, doubt, and nostalgia for the great certitudes. The distinctiveness of values led not only to moral autonomy, aesthetic exaltation, and the free search for truth but also to demoralization, frivolous estheticism, and nihilism. The erstwhile rejuvenating virtue of the idea of the new (new = better = necessary = progress) was exhausting itself and was typically reserved for detergents, television screens, and automobile performance. There could no longer be a "new novel," "new cuisine," or a "new philosophy."

If consciousness of the ambivalence of all the processes developed by, and which developed, modernity was in evidence in the West, the critique of modernity, far from overcoming it, was the result of an impoverished postmodernism that was incapable of conceiving tomorrow.

Henceforth, the feeling, sometimes diffuse, sometimes more pronounced, that the future has been lost is common. There has been a general consciousness that we are not in the next to last stage of history, awaiting the day of fulfillment. There has been a general sense that we are not heading toward a radiant, nor even a happy, tomorrow. However, what has been and is still lacking is the consciousness that we are now in the Planetary Iron Age—the prehistory of the human spirit.

The sickness of the future has insinuated itself into the present and induced psychological distress, especially when a civilization's faith capital is invested in the future.

Living day to day can deaden the feeling of this crisis of the future and make it so that, despite the uncertainties, one goes on entertaining private hopes, bringing children into the world and planning for their future.

At the same time, the crisis of the future sets in motion a massive backflow to the past, even more so to the extent that the present is miserable, anxious, and unhappy. The past, which had been ruined by the future, now rises from the ruins of the future. Thus we see a tremendous and multiform movement of rerooting, of return to lost or forgotten ethnic, national, and religious foundations, out of which arise various "fundamentalisms."[7]

The effects of these pendulum swings and sudden turnarounds between past and future are far from being played out, and many of them will be unforeseen.

In any case, progress is not automatically guaranteed by any law of history. The passage of time is not necessarily equivalent to development. Henceforth, the future spells uncertainty.

The Tragedy of Development

Development is the master word, adopted by the United Nations, upon which all the popular ideologies of the second half of this century converged. At the base of the master idea of development stands the great Western paradigm of progress. Development is supposed to insure progress, which in turn is supposed to insure development.

There are two sides to development. On the one hand, there is a global myth wherein societies, having become industrialized, attain well-being, reduce their extreme inequalities, and dispense to individuals the maximum amount of happiness that a society is capable of dispensing. On the other hand, development is a reductionistic conception which holds that economic growth is the necessary and sufficient condition for all social, psychological, and moral developments. This techno-economic conception ignores the human problems of identity, community, solidarity, and culture.

---

[7]The years 1977-80 are an important turning point: In 1977, secular Zionism gave way to a Biblical Israelism with the coming of Begin to power. In 1978, John-Paul II was elected Pope and initiated the reevangelization of the world. In 1979, a more or less secular Iran fell under the power of the Ayatollah Khomeiny.

Thus, the notion of development is sorely underdeveloped. This underdevelopment is a poor and abstract product of the poor and abstract notion of development.

Bound to blind faith in the irresistible forward march of progress, the blind faith in development allowed, on the one hand, for the elimination of doubts and, on the other, for the obscuring of the barbarities set in motion by the development of development.

The myth of development called for the belief that everything had to be sacrificed to it. It made possible the justification of pitiless dictatorships, whether of the "socialist" (single party) or pro-Western (military dictatorship) type. The cruelties of the revolutions of development aggravated the tragedies of underdevelopment.

After 30 years devoted to development, the great North/South imbalance remains, and inequalities are worsening. Twenty-five percent of the world's population, living in the rich countries, consumes seventy-five percent of the energy. The great powers retain a monopoly on high technology and even possess a cognitive and manipulative power over the genetic material of living species, including the human. The developed world destroys its agricultural surplus and lets its land lie fallow while droughts and famines multiply in the world of the poor. When civil wars or natural disasters strike, temporary charitable aid is devoured by bureaucratic or opportunistic parasites. The Third World continues to suffer economic exploitation from the developed world, but also from its blindness, closed-mindedness, and moral and intellectual underdevelopment.

In Africa, the soil is overworked, the climate is being degraded, the population is increasing, and AIDS is devastating the continent. A polyculture keyed to familial and local needs is being replaced by a monoculture subjected to the hazards of the global market. Hit by these hazards, this monoculture suffers crisis after crisis; capital flees the sectors in crisis. The rural exodus fills shantytowns with the unemployed. The monetarization and commodification of everything destroys the communitarian life of conviviality and services rendered, and the best of indigenous cultures disappears to the benefit of the worst of Western civilization.

The idea of development was and is blind to the cultural riches of archaic societies that have only been viewed through economistic and quantitative glasses. All that has been seen in such cultures is false ideas, ignorance, and superstitions, without even imagining that they contained profound intuitions, knowledge gathered over the centuries, and life-wisdom and ethical values that have been let to atrophy. Under the influence of Western-centered rationalization, proponents of developmentalism have also been blind to the fact that the cultures of our developed societies include, like all societies, but in their own ways, considerable vices alongside their undeniable virtues. Among the latter is a self-critical rationality that allows for the highlighting of gaps and faults in our own culture. Among the former, however, are arbitrary ideas, unfounded myths (including the providentialist myth of progress), grand illusions (including the illusion of having arrived at the summit of rationality and of being the sole possessors of the same), and terrific blindspots (such as fragmented, compartmentalized, reductionistic, and mechanistic thinking).

From its European beginnings, the development of urban and industrialized modernity has involved the destruction of centuries-old rural cultures and has started to attack the fabric of various regional cultures, which, to varying degrees, are offering some resistance. Among the great historical cultures of Asia and the Muslim world, there has been resistance to Westernization, at times through the assumption of a dual identity (Japan, Morocco), at others through a regeneration of a religious and ethnic base. As noted earlier, resistance to Westernization proceeds through the appropriation of Western aims and instruments: the formula for the nation-state; industrial, administrative, and military techniques; and the emancipatory ideology of the sovereignty of the people.

This appropriation leads, through the same process, to a double movement of rerooting in the past and being catapulted into the future. A complex dynamic is set in motion, wherein identity/religion/nation/State/technology all interact, and wherein capitalism, Western ideologies, revolutionary ideology, and mass culture all play a part, giving rise to rebellion, hope, then resignation, despair, and renewed rebellion. All of this does not happen without convulsions, internal conflict, and bastard compromises. In any case, Westernization proceeds through technification, commodification, commercialization, and ideologization, while, on the contrary, as discussed earlier, there is an ongoing balkanization and rerooting of ethnoreligious identity.

In the rest of the world, development tends to complete the disintegration of archaic cultures that had already begun during the historical period and was pursued massively through colonization. The world of indigenous cultures, now reduced to 300 million people, is bound to disappear.

We are witnessing the ultimate phase in the annihilation of hunter-gatherer cultures, which still survive in the tropical forests, forbidding mountains, and desert reaches. Medical progress brings them hygiene and healing, but also eliminates practices and remedies of the indigenous healers or shamans. Literacy brings written culture, but destroys the oral traditions along with age-old knowledge and wisdom. Traditional personality types are also dismantled.

The recent experiment in James Bay illustrates this process. Following the logic of development, Hydro-Québec undertook the construction of large dams, destined to furnish cheap electricity to the province and, at the same time, to attract the creation of aluminum factories. Part of the land was bought from the Cree Indians, which gave them the means to lead a sedentary life, to acquire houses and household appliances, to adopt and adapt to work/energy/growth, and so on. However, in the lands acquired by Hydro-Québec, the creation of artificial lakes cut off the migratory routes of the caribou, and the freeing of mercury by their waters made the fish inedible. The men, forced to abandon their formerly vital hunting and fishing, went to work on the construction of the dams and then became unemployed upon the dam's completion. The elderly, now inactive, resigned themselves to death. The young succumbed to alcoholism; even four-year olds were seen drunk on beer. The women, who went immediately from meat and fish to starchy foods and sweets, have become obese. The old community was destroyed and a new one had not been constructed in its place. Altruism had given way to egoism. An ancient way of life, an ancient world of life, was dead. Domestic well-being had arrived, and with it alcoholism, drugs, and boredom. The Cree are now rich in goods and poor in spirit, unhappy and on the road to extinction.

In every case, including Europe but more seriously outside of Europe, development destroys, more or less rapidly, local solidarities and original traits adapted to specific ecological conditions.

One must not, of course, idealize cultures. One must recognize that all evolutions involve leaving something behind, that all creation involves destruction, and that every historical gain is paid for with a loss. One must understand that, as everything that lives is bound to die, each culture is worthy of living but must know how to die. We must also maintain the necessity for a planetary culture. It is true that the multiplicity of cultures, with their marvellous adaptation to local conditions and problems, stand as obstacles to the attainment of a planetary culture. Yet can we not extract from each one and generalize the richness of what each has to offer? How then can we integrate the values and treasures of cultures in the process of disintegration? Is it not too late? We therefore have to come to terms with two contradictory injunctions: to save the extraordinary cultural diversity created by the human diaspora and, at the same time, to nourish a planetary culture common to us all. From an another angle, we can see that, parallel to the process of cultural homogenization propelled by the spread of techno-industrial civilization, there is also a process of cultural encounter and syncretism: The United States, Latin America, and Africa are home to an ongoing creation of cultural diversity. This in no way, however, diminishes the fact that techno-industrial development continues to threaten the entire world.

Everywhere there is generalized technicization, industrialization, and urbanization, and we do not know which among their ambivalent effects will prevail. All of this is bringing about a full-speed destruction of agrarian cultures and the end of an age-old rural world: Whereas 3% of the world population lived in cities in 1800, 80% of the European West do so today. Megalopolises like Mexico, Shanghai, Bombay, Jakarta, and Tokyo-Osaka continue to expand. These urban monsters, along with their inhabitants, suffer from traffic jams, noise, stress, and pollution of all kinds. Material misery is proliferating in the shanty towns, and moral misery is not confined to drug- and-crime-infested neighborhoods; such misery also reigns in the luxurious neighborhoods protected by militia and bodyguards.

United Nations demographers predict that, around the year 2000, more than 50% of the world's population will live in urban settings, and 60 megalopolises will contain more than 650 million people, that is, 8.3% of the world's population will occupy one half of a thousandth of the planet's dry land. Among the 21 megalopolises of more than 10 million inhabitants, 17 will be from poor countries.

Where is global development heading? Some underdeveloped countries are heading toward disaster; others, having freed themselves from economic underdevelopment, will find themselves saddled with the problems of the developed world. The latter, for its part, is already home to the development of economic underdevelopment: 35 million human beings live below the poverty line in the United States alone. It appears that we are entering a "dual" society that banishes to the ghettos those excluded from development, including 10% to 20% unemployed.

Are we heading toward a global crisis of development? In any case, we must reject the underdeveloped concept of development that made techno-industrial growth the panacea of all anthroposocial development and renounce the mythological idea of an irresistible progress extending to infinity.

The Dis-ease of Civilization

Is not our civilization, the very model of development, itself sick because of development?

The development of our civilization has produced marvels: the domestication of physical energy, increasingly automated and intelligent industrial machines, appliances that liberate households from the most menial tasks, well-being, comfort, an extreme variety of consumer goods, the automobile (which, as the word indicates, gives autonomy combined with mobility), the airplane through which we overcome great distances, and television providing an open window to real and imaginary worlds.

This development has permitted individual unfolding, intimacy in love and friendship, communication between "you" and "me," and telecommunication between all and sundry. Yet this same development also brings the atomization of individuals, who lose their old solidarities without acquiring new ones, except for those of an anonymous and administrative nature.

The development of the technobureaucratic era introduces a generalization of fragmented work without initiative, responsibility, or interest. Clock time, racing forward, does away with availability, with calm and natural rhythms. Hurriedness chases away reflection and meditation. The bureaucratic/technological/industrial megamachine encompasses an ever-greater number of activities, forcing people to comply with its prescriptions, injunctions, and formulas. One cannot dialogue with such anonymous forces. We are at a loss as to how to correct their errors. We do not know the office or window to which we should address ourselves. Mechanization takes control of the nonmechanical. Concrete existence is obscured. The anonymous rule of money goes hand in hand with the anonymous rule of technobureaucracy. That which stimulates also disintegrates: The spirit of competition and success develops egoism and dissolves solidarity.

The city of light, which offers freedom and variety, is also the urban sprawl whose constraints, beginning with the daily treadmill of going to and from work, eating and sleeping, stifles existence and exhausts the nervous system through accumulated stress.

Democratic living is regressing. The more problems acquire a technical dimension, the more they fall outside the average citizen's competence and into the hands of the experts. The more the problems of civilization become political, the less politicians are able to integrate them into their language and programs.

Production is subordinate to consumption, and the latter to products sold on the market, which in turn are subordinated to libidinal forces less and less controlled within the circular process that creates a consumer for the product, not just a product for the consumer. A superficial agitation takes hold of individuals the moment they escape the enslaving constraints of work. Unchecked consumption turns into bulimic overconsumption, which alternates with curative privations. The obsession with dieting and keeping a slim figure multiplies narcissistic fears and food crazes and feeds the costly cult of vitamins and other supplements. Among the rich, consumption becomes hysterical. People are obsessed with status, the best labels, beauty, a good complexion, and health. There is much window shopping and touring of department stores, antique shops, and flea markets, and a mindless accumulation of knick-knacks and curios.

People live from day to day, consuming the present, fascinated by a thousand futilities, lost in endless chatter and mutual incomprehension in the Tower of Bagatelles. Incapable of standing still, they fly off in every direction. Tourism is less a discovery of the "other," a physical relating to the planet, than it is a somnambulistic guided tour through a semifantastic world of folklore and monuments. Modern "entertainment" barely hides the void it attempts to flee.

The rise in the standard of living, moreover, can be linked to the degradation of the quality of life. The multiplication of the means of communication can be linked to the impoverishment of personal communication. Individuals can be simultaneously autonomous and atomized sovereigns and objects, masters of their machines and manipulated/enslaved by what they master.

At the same time, something is threatening our civilization from the inside. The degradation of personal relationships, solitude, and the loss of certainty, combined with the inability to face uncertainty, nourishes an increasingly widespread subjective disease. Because this spiritual disease is lodged in our depths, because it manifests itself psychosomatically in insomnia, respiratory problems, stomach ulcers, and other more vague complaints, we do not see its cultural and collective dimension, and we turn to physicians, psychotherapists, or gurus.

When adolescence rebels against society, when it "tunes out" and turns on to hard drugs, we believe that the problem lies with the kids. We do not see that adolescence is the weak link in the chain of civilization, that it concentrates within itself the problems, the hurt, and the aspirations elsewhere diffused and atomized. The search for autonomy along with community, the need for an authentic relationship to nature wherein we rediscover our own nature, and the rejection of the adulterated life of adults, reveals through negation the privations suffered by us all. The call for peace and love of Californian adolescents in the 1960s betrayed a deep distress of the soul.

The protests of 1968 revealed an adolescent challenge to the very principles of life in the Western world, a life both psychically and morally miserable, despite its material prosperity.

Objective evils that come from economic difficulties or dysfunctions, bureaucratic heavy-handedness and rigidity, and ecological degradation have become increasingly perceptible and are starting to be spoken about and spoken against. Yet the evils of civilization that infiltrate the soul and take shape subjectively are not always perceived. In any case, objective and subjective evils meet to form a new disease of civilization. Appearing in the West in and through economic development, it will continue in and through economic crisis.

The imaginary world evoked by the media took up this malaise beginning in 1968. Before this time, commercial films all had a happy ending, and the heroes of popular literature found success and love by the end of the story. Women's magazines distributed recipes for happiness. After 1968, happiness was a problem and no longer a euphoric myth. The happy ending was not a foregone conclusion. Women's magazines counseled their readers on how courageously to face the problems of separation, solitude, sickness, or old age.

One should note that "civil society" also reacted and tried to protect itself through its own means. Thus, a counter to the constraints of urban bureaucratized living began to manifest itself as of the 1960s with the development of a life style alternating between work and relaxation, the city and the country, with weekends and multiple vacations. A neo-archaism and a neonaturalism filled interiors with plants, shells, stones, and fossils, led to the wearing of jeans, velvet, countrified clothes, and primitive jewelry, and brought barbecues, garden vegetables, and hearty stews back into fashion. Soon after, the rise in ecological consciousness stressed the search for everything "natural," especially food.

Eros, which can assume, both separately and simultaneously, the face of love, eroticism, sexuality, and friendship, is the fundamental counter to the dis-ease of civilization, a counter that civilization itself calls forth and broadcasts through its media. Resistance to anonymization and atomization manifests itself, especially among the youth, through the multiplication of rallying symbols for tribes, groups of friends, and parties. Furthermore, for people of all ages, love has become the saviour god. Marriage, once a form of alliance between families, is scarcely conceivable now without love. The dis-ease of the soul is repressed by the impetus of love, which is born and reborn everywhere. Amorous and erotic encounters cut across social classes, defy interdictions, and thrive on the clandestine and precarious.

However, consuming passions quickly consume themselves; love weakens as it multiplies and becomes more fragile with time.

Meetings that give birth to new love kill the old. Couples split apart, others come together, only to split again. The disease of instability, of hurriedness, of superficiality, infects love itself and brings back the disease of civilization, which love chases away.

Love and fellowship, spontaneous forces of resistance against the dis-ease of civilization, are still too weak to be its cure. They chase away emptiness through their striving for wholeness, but they are themselves gnawed at and eaten away by this emptiness, from which arises a complex of emptiness/wholeness, the nature of which is very difficult to grasp.

Finally, there are other forms of resistance to the dis-ease of civilization, notable among which is the desire to assimilate the methods and messages of Oriental cultures that speak of harmony of body, mind, and spirit, and of spiritual detachment. It is in this sense that the popularized and commercialized forms of yoga and Zen reveal the deficiencies of Western civilization and the needs being addressed. At the same time, under the guise of diverse syncretistic religiosities, including New Age philosophy, there is a search for the unity of the true, the good, and the beautiful, for the restoration of communion and the sacred. There is, amidst the ruins of everything destroyed by progress—which is itself henceforth in ruins—a quest for lost truths.

It is very difficult to recognize the true nature of the dis-ease of civilization, given its ambivalences and complexities. One must see the collapsed foundations, the caves, the subterranean chasms, and at the same time the will to life and the muted and unconscious struggle against the dis-ease. One must see the complex of dehumanization and rehumanization. One must see the satisfactions, joys, pleasures, and happiness, but also the dissatisfaction, sufferings, frustrations, anxieties, and unhappiness of the developed world, which differ, but are no less real, than those of the underdeveloped world. That which is caught up in a vital struggle against the death of this civilization is also part of this civilization. The neuroses that it provokes are not merely an effect of the disease, but also a more or less painful compromise with the disease so as to avoid succumbing completely to it.

Are these reactions to the disease insufficient? Will it get worse? In any case, our civilization cannot be thought of as having attained a stable condition. Having liberated unheard of forces of destruction, is it heading toward self-destruction or its metamorphosis?

The Uncontrolled and Blind Development of Technoscience

Our times are more than ever animated by the dual dynamic of the development of the sciences and that of technology, each of which is nourished by the other. This dynamic propels industrial and civilizational development across the globe and is stimulated by it in return. Thus technoscience has led the world for the last century. Its developments and expansions have driven the development and expansion of communications, interdependence, solidarities, reorganizations, and homogenizations which themselves develop the Planetary Era. Yet it is also these developments and expansions that provoke, through positive/negative feedback, the balkanizations, heterogenizations, disorganizations, and crises of the present.

Faith in the providential mission of technoscience nourished the certainty of progress and the grandiose hopes of future development.

Technoscience is not merely the locomotive of the Planetary Era. It has invaded every tissue of the developed societies, implanting at an organizational level the logic of the artificial machine. This logic has penetrated the sphere of daily life and repressed the democratic power of citizens in favor of the experts and specialists. It has processed thought through its impositions of disjunctions and reductions.

Technoscience is thus both nucleus and motor of the planetary struggle.

Invasion by the Logic of the Artificial Machine

What is it that distinguishes an artificial machine from a living one?[8]

Artificial machines are composed of extremely reliable elements. However, the machine as a whole is much less reliable than each of its elements taken in isolation. All it takes is a local alteration for the whole thing to become jammed and out of order, and the machine cannot be repaired without some external intervention. Artificial machines can neither tolerate nor integrate disorder. They are strictly bound to their own programs. They are made of highly specialized elements and are devoted to specialized tasks. It is only recently that computers have given them a general intelligence applicable to a variety of problems.

The living machine, for its part, is constituted of largely unreliable elements that degrade rapidly (proteins), but the whole is much more reliable than its elements. It is capable of producing new constituents to replace those that degrade (molecules) or die (cells)

---

[8]For Morin (1981), "every physical being whose activity includes work, transformation, production can be conceived as a machine" (p. 156). Artificial machines are merely the last in a long line of "machine-beings," beginning with the Sun and including the Earth itself, its organisms, and anthroposocial organizations.

and is thus able to regenerate itself; it is able to repair itself when injured locally. If death is the enemy of living organization, its destructive forces are used in a way that permits regeneration. Although the artificial machine is bound to a program, the living machine is capable of strategy, that is, it can invent behaviors in the midst of uncertainty and randomness. There is thus, in the living machine, a consubstantial and complex link between disorganization and reorganization, disorder and creativity.

Moreover, the living machine consists not only of specialized but of multifunctional organs. Its generative (genetic) system includes not only specialized genes, but polyvalent genes within groups of genes that are themselves polyvalent. The artificial machine is only a machine. The living machine is also an auto-eco-organizing being—an individual/subject.

All these qualities of the living machine being are raised to their highest pitch in human beings, in which subjectivity and the ability to choose (freedom) come into full bloom.

When applied to humans, the logic of the artificial machine develops the program to the detriment of strategy, hyperspecialization to the detriment of general competence, and mechanicity to the detriment of organizational complexity: strict functionality, rationalization, and chronometrization that impose obedience to the organization of the artificial machine. The latter ignores the living individual and its quality of being a subject and, thus, ignores human subjective realities.

The logic of the artificial machine imposes itself initially in industry which, although liberating human muscles from heavy tasks, subjugated the worker to its mechanistic and specialized norms as well as to its chronometric time. The artificial machine, although subjected to human needs, at the same time subjugated human beings to its mechanical needs. Created as an appendage of human activity, it made the worker an appendage of its own.

The logic of the artificial machine spread beyond the industrial sector, notably in the world of administration, in which this logic had already been prefigured in bureaucratic organization. It took hold of numerous domains of social activity: as Gideon (1948) put it, mechanization took command. To begin with, it had become master of the urban world, then of the rural, where it transformed peasants into farmers and suburbanized towns and villages.

The logic of the artificial machine—efficiency, predictability, calculability, rigid specialization, speed, chronometric time—invaded everyday life: It regulated travel, consumption, leisure, education, the food and service industries, and brought about what George Ritzer calls the "Macdonaldization of society."

Urbanization, atomization, and anonymization go hand in hand with the generalized application of the logic of the artificial machine to human beings and their relations. The notion of development that has imposed itself on the planet obeys the logic of the artificial machine.

Thus, taking possession of technology is simultaneously a possession by technology. We think we are rationalizing society for human beings, but we are in fact rationalizing human beings to adapt them to the rationalization of society.

The Rule of Mechanistic and Fragmented Thinking

The extension of the logic of the artificial machine to every aspect of life produces mechanistic and fragmented thinking that takes technocratic and econocratic form. Such thinking perceives only mechanical causality while everything increasingly obeys a complex causality. It reduces reality to that which is quantifiable. Hyperspecialization and reduction to the quantifiable produce a blindness not only to existence, the concrete, and the individual, but also to context, the global, and the fundamental. They involve, in all technobureaucratic systems, a fragmenting, a dilution, and finally a loss of responsibility. They favor rigidities in action along with a laxity of indifference. They contribute strongly to the regression of democracy in Western countries, where all problems, having become technical, elude the grasp of citizens to the profit of the experts, and where the loss of global and fundamental vision gives free reign not only to the most closed and fragmented ideas, but also to the most hollow of global ideas and the most arbitrary fundamental ideas, including and especially those of the technicians and scientists themselves.

The ravages of a closed and fragmented rationality are manifest in the conception of great technobureaucratic projects that always forget about one or several dimensions of the problem at hand (as with the Aswan dam in Egypt, the installation of Fos-sur-Mer in Southern France, the organization CNTS and the case of contaminated blood, the project to divert Siberian rivers, etc.). In fact, closed rationality produces irrationality. It is obviously incapable of facing the challenge of planetary problems.

The New Barbarism

There are forms of human suffering that result from natural cataclysms, droughts, floods, and famines. There are others that result from long-standing barbarisms that have not lost their virulence. Yet there are those, finally, that result from a new technoscientific-bureaucratic barbarism, itself inseparable from the hold that the logic of the artificial machine has on human beings.

Science is not only elucidating, it is also blind to its own process, and its fruit, as with the biblical tree of knowledge, contains seeds of both good and evil. Along with civilization, technology brings a new barbarism that is both anonymous and manipulative. The word of reason signifies not only critical rationality, but also the logical delirium of rationalization with its blindness to concrete beings and the complexity of reality. What we take to be advances in civilization are at the same time advances in barbarism.

Walter Benjamin (1970) correctly saw that there is barbarism at the source of the great civilizations. Freud (1930) correctly saw that civilization, far from superseding barbarism by repressing it into its depths, was preparing new eruptions of it. We must see in our own day that technoscientific civilization, while remaining civilization, produces its own kind of barbarism.

The Powerlessness to Bring About a Metatechnological Mutation

The myth of progress is collapsing, development is sick; all existing threats to the whole of humanity have at least some of their causes in the development of science and technology (the threat from mass destruction, ecological threats to the biosphere, population explosion).

Yet technoscientific developments might themselves allow, in this turn of the millennium, for the recovery of general abilities; the replacement of hyperspecialized work by robots, machines, and computers; the organization of a distributive economy to do away with dearth and famine in the Third World and to integrate the excluded; and the replacement of rigid systems of instruction with an education in complexity.

A metatechnological civilization is conceivable, precisely with the help and integration of technology, with the control of the current logic of artificial machines by human norms, and with the progressive introduction of a complex logic—which is just beginning to happen—into computers and, through this route, into the world of artificial machines.

The powerlessness to bring about the great technological/ economic/social mutation lies not only in the inadequacy of technological and economic knowledge, but also in the deficiency of the dominant techno-econocratic way of thinking. It lies also in the debility of political thinking, which, since the collapse of Marxism, is incapable of putting complex thinking into practice and of envisioning a grand design. There is a powerlessness to escape the crisis of modernity through anything but an impoverished postmodernism.

Racing Blindly Forward

The threefold race in science/technology/industry that has taken over the human adventure is now out of control: Growth is out of control, its progress leading to the abyss.

The euphoric vision of Bacon, Descartes, and Marx, wherein humanity, as masters of technology, were to become masters of nature, gives way to the vision of Heisenberg and Gehlen (see Morin 1969), wherein humanity becomes the instrument of a metabiological development driven by technology. We must abandon the two major myths of the modern West: the conquest of nature-as-object by humans—the sole subjects of the universe—and the false infinite toward which industrial growth hurled itself, with its notions of development and progress. We must abandon partial and closed rationalities, along with abstract and delirious rationalizations that consider as irrational all attempts to subject them to a rational critique. We must deliver ourselves from the pseudorational paradigm of *homo sapiens faber* within which science and technology take charge of and accomplish human development.

The tragedy of development and the underdevelopment of development, the frantic race of technoscience, and the blindness produced by fragmented and reductionistic thinking, has thrown us into an uncontrolled adventure.

A LIFE AND DEATH STRUGGLE

Crisis?

One could consider the chaos and conflict of the Planetary Era to be its "normal" state, its disorders to be the inevitable ingredients of its complexity, and so avoid using the term *crisis*, which, these days, has become banal and something of a buzz word.

Perhaps we should recall what is to be understood by *crisis* (Morin, 1994). A crisis manifests itself through an increase, or rather a generalization, of uncertainties through ruptures in regulation or negative feedback (which neutralize deviations), by the development of positive feedback (uncontrolled growth), or by an increase in perils and opportunities (perils of regression or death, opportunities to find solutions or salvation).

When we consider the state of the planet, we see the following:

- Mounting uncertainties in all domains, the impossibility of any assured futurology, the extreme diversity of possible future scenarios;
- The rupture of regulating factors (including, recently, the rupture of the "balance of terror"); the development of rising positive feedback, as in population growth; the uncontrolled developments of industrial growth and of technoscience;
- Deadly perils facing the whole of humanity (nuclear arms, threat to the biosphere) and, at the same time, the opportunity to save humanity from these perils, starting with the consciousness of these very perils.

The Polycrisis

It would be beneficial to be able to hierarchize "crisical" problems so as to concentrate attention on the foremost or major problem.

In one sense, the uncontrolled adventure of technoscience is the major problem: It dominates the problem of development and that of civilization; it has influenced the population surge and the ecological threat. Yet to control today the march of technoscience would not *ipso facto* resolve the tragedy of development or the problematic character of our civilization; it would not lift the blindness produced by fragmented and reductionistic thinking and would suppress neither the population problem nor the ecological threat. Moreover, the problem of technoscience depends on the whole of the civilization that now depends on it. It cannot be treated in isolation and must be seen from many angles according to the regions of the planet.

In fact, there are inter-retroactions between the different problems, crises, and threats. Such is also the case for the problems of health, population, the environment, lifestyle, civilization, and development. So it is also with the crisis of the future, which promotes virulent nationalisms, economic instability, and general balkanization, all of this through inter-retroactions. From a wider perspective, the crisis of the anthroposphere and that of the biosphere are mutually implicative, as are the crises of the past, present, and future.

Many of these crises can themselves be looked on as polycrisical sets of interwoven and overlapping crises: So it is with the crisis of development, the crisis of all societies, in which some are shaken from their lethargy, their autarchy, and their immobility, and others accelerate at a dizzying pace, carried forward to a blind tomorrow, and moved by the dialectic of the developments of technoscience and the outbreak of human deliria.

Thus one is at a loss to single out a number one problem to which all others would be subordinated. There is no single vital problem, but many vital problems, and it is this complex intersolidarity of problems, antagonisms, crises, uncontrolled processes, and the general crisis of the planet that constitutes the number one vital problem.

The Acceleration

The gravity or the depth of the crisis can be measured by the degree of positive feedback and the importance of deadly perils.

To be sure, the whole techno-economic history of the West since the end of the 18th century can be seen as a gigantic process of positive feedback, that is, as an uncontrolled, self-nourishing, self-amplifying, and self-accelerating process that destructures traditional societies, along with their ways of living and their cultures. This process of destruction has, at the same time, been one of creation (of a civilization, new cultural forms, poetry, music, etc).

The question today is that of knowing whether the forces of regression and destruction will overtake those of progression and creation, and whether we have crossed a critical threshold in the process of acceleration/amplification that could lead to an explosive runaway.

Acceleration is overtaking all sectors of life. The rate of change is itself accelerating. Through technological acceleration, with faxes, high-speed trains, express delivery, and supersonic jets, we ourselves are accelerated. A whole civilization is caught in a mad rush forward.

We must raise to consciousness this insane rush forward that has less and less the appearance of progress, or which rather is the other face of progress. As Walter Benjamin (1970) said, speaking of the Angel dragged forward by a raging storm: "This storm is what we call progress" (p. 260).

Are we therefore running toward self-destruction? Toward a mutation?

Runaway positive feedback can, potentially, produce a mutation, but this would require that the forces of control and regulation gain the upper hand.

It is a question, then, of curbing the rule of technology over cultures, civilization, and nature, insofar as this rule poses a threat to them. It is a question of slowing down to avoid either an explosion, or an implosion. It is a question of decelerating enough to be able to regulate, control, and prepare the mutation. Survival calls for a revolutionizing transformation. We must create the conditions for a different tomorrow. Such must be the overarching concern of the new millennium.

The Damoclean Phase

The planetary crisis is at the heart of existing uncontrolled processes, and the latter are at the heart of the planetary crisis. One of the characteristics of this crisis is the rise in deadly global threats.

The bomb dropped on Hiroshima in 1945 began a new phase, in which the nuclear threat is forever suspended above the whole of humanity. This Damoclean situation came about with the creation of enormous arsenals capable of destroying the human race several times over, with megadeath missiles hidden by the thousands in underground silos, cutting through the oceans in nuclear submarines, flying without stop in superbombers. Nuclear weapons are spreading, becoming miniaturized, and may soon be in the hands of demented potentates and/or terrorists.

At the same time, the Damoclean threat has spread to the biosphere, where the waste products and other emissions of our techno-urban development threaten death through the poisoning of our ecosystem.

So, too, death, repressed though medicine and hygiene, has reinfected our sexuality with a hitherto unheard of virulence, threatening each embrace with the Damoclean spectre.

Finally, accompanied by anxiety, despair, and violence, death has gained a foothold within the psyche itself. The forces of destruction and self-destruction, latent in each individual and society, have been reactivated in our anonymous urban milieus, multiplying and amplifying the solitude and anxiety of individuals, disinhibiting a violence that becomes the banal expression of protest, rejection, and revolt. The deadly appeal of hard drugs, especially heroin, is spreading irresistibly; these drugs pacify, intoxicate, and excite, but the heaven they offer is a heaven of death.

From the very emergence of *homo sapiens*, all human beings have harbored the consciousness of their own death and of those they hold dear. With the fall of the Roman empire came the idea that civilizations are mortal. For a century now, and more compellingly with the findings of modern cosmology, the knowledge has spread that the Earth and the Sun themselves will die, dragging life along with them. But to these already envisioned deaths must be added new, more intimate ones, new global deaths, a looming, enveloping, empoisoning series of deaths weighing on the planet as a whole.

The Alliance of Barbarisms

It is precisely in this, our Damoclean phase, that one sees the cresting of multiple waves, on numerous points of the globe, of a great barbarism spawned from the alliance of old, ever virulent forms of barbarism (fanaticisms, cruelties, contempt, hatred, all more than ever nourished by religions, racisms, nationalisms, ideologies) with newer, anonymous, cold, bureaucratic, technoscientific forms of barbarism that have been developed in our own century. The multiform alliance between these two barbarisms, sealed at Kolyma, Auschwitz, and Hiroshima, has henceforth become universal in its threat to the survival and further evolution of humanity.

A Life-and-Death Struggle?

If one considers together the two crisical and critical cyclones of the two World Wars of the 20th century along with the unknown cyclone in the process of formation, if one considers the deadly threats that humanity has brought on itself, and if, finally and especially, one considers the current situation of overlapping and indissociable crises, we see the planetary crisis of a humanity still incapable of realizing itself as humanity. Humanity is caught in a tragic and uncertain struggle in which symptoms of death and birth wrestle and fuse with one another. A dead past refuses to die, and a future is stuck in the throws of its labor.

The world is being swept by blind forces, by runaway positive feedback, by suicidal folly. However, there is also the globalization of the call for peace, democracy, freedom, and tolerance.

The struggle between the forces of integration and disintegration is being played out not only in the relations between societies, nations, ethnic groups, and religions, but also at the heart of each society and in the heart of every individual. It is not merely a question of a struggle between civilizing and barbaric influences, but also a struggle between the collective hope for survival and the risks of collective death. Such is our present struggle, without, however, it necessarily being the final struggle that will bring us out of the Planetary Iron Age.

All of the old immunities, which formerly protected cultures, are now working both against and for humanity. They work to maintain diversity, but also to impede unity. National immunities have become more destructive than protective. Humanity has yet, as a planetary entity, to acquire any kind of immunity against the afflictions that ravage it from within.

The life-and-death struggle of the planet is not simply the sum of traditional conflicts of all against each, plus the various kinds of crisis, plus the emergence of new problems without a solution. *It is a totality that feeds on conflictual, crisical, and problematical ingredients, a totality that envelops, outstrips, and feeds them in return.*

This totality contains the problem of problems: the inability of the world to become a world, the inability of humanity to become humanity.

Are we irremediably engaged in a race to a generalized cataclysm? To what will this troubled, multiple labor give birth? Or will we continue to limp along toward a planetary Dark Age, with its regional conflicts, successive crises, disorders, and regressions—along with perhaps a few protected islands.

The death/birth struggle is perhaps the way, through infinite risks, toward the general metamorphosis—on the condition that we raise to consciousness this very struggle.

4

Our Earth-Centered Goals

In order to realize humanity and civilize the Earth, we must become aware of our earthly roots and our planetary destiny. Thus, the recovery of our earthly roots is in itself a goal. Everything is connected: in order to set up our earth-centered goals, we must understand and acknowledge our cosmic *Dasein,* our earthly identity, our anthropological condition, and that of the Planetary Iron Age.

TO PRESERVE, TO CHANGE

Two apparently antagonistic goals should henceforth be inseparably linked: first, the survival of humanity, and second, ongoing hominization.

The first goal is conservative as it aims at preserving and safeguarding not only cultural and natural diversities defaced by unrelenting processes of standardization and destruction, or civilizational gains threatened by barbarous regressions and outbursts, but also the very life of humanity threatened by nuclear weaponry and biospheric pollution, a Damoclean double threat that is a product of Hyperbarbarism. This great barbarism, as may be recalled, arises from a combination of forces, including those that, rampant since the beginning of human history, spell domination, violence, and hatred, along with the modern technobureaucratic forces that, anonymously and coldly, undo both humanity and nature.

The second goal is revolutionizing (I purposely avoid the word *revolutionary,* which has become *reactionary* and is tarnished by barbarism) and aims at creating the conditions within which humanity could realize itself as such in a community/society of nations. This new stage will only be reached if human relations are everywhere revolutionized, from those of the self with itself, between the self and others or between relatives, to those between nations and states, between people and the technobureaucracy, between individuals and societies, between knowers and knowledge, and between human beings and nature.

An unavoidable paradox ensues. To preserve involves change in order to guarantee the pursuit of hominization. To change requires conservation, not only of our biological integrity, but of our cultural and civilizational legacies as well.

TO RESIST

A second paradox lies under the seemingly contradictory double imperative: to preserve/to change, namely, to progress/to resist.

Resistance is a duty that has persisted even after 1944; after France's liberation from German occupation, resistance was directed against Stalinist totalitarianism. Personally, I am proud of having done just that after having fought against Nazism. Beyond totalitarianism and again in very different ways, resistance is still needed.

To resist means to behave defensively on all fronts against possible returns or floods of hyperbarbarism. The idea of resistance is not limited to opposing foreign occupants or merciless dictatorship. The People's Spring of 1989-1990 has frozen back into winter, its seeds of freedom being destroyed. Meanwhile the great barbarism is making a comeback.

To be sure, always and everywhere, humanity has had to resist pervading cruelty and attendant spite, contempt, and indifference. Yet the present-day twofold barbarism stands for excessively heightened cruelty: heinous cruelty stems from the first barbarism and issues into murder, torture, individual, and collective furor; and anonymous cruelty stems from technobureaucratic barbarism. Thoroughly illustrative of this, the contaminated blood incident shows how the second barbarism typically combines technicization, hyperspecialization, compartmentalization, bureaucratization, anonymity, abstraction, and commodification, all of which together lead to the loss not only of what is global and fundamental, but also what is responsible or what is concrete and human.

To resist the twofold barbarism has consequently become a primordial and vital necessity, a condition for the survival of humanity, a prerequisite to ongoing hominization. In this way, we are driven simultaneously to resist, preserve, and change. Hence there is the connection that was inconceivable not so long ago:

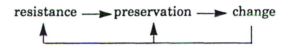

THE CONSCIOUS PURSUIT OF HOMINIZATION

The conscious pursuit of hominization would bring about a new birth of humanity. The first birth took place at the beginning of hominization. The second was the fruit of emerging language and culture, probably as early as *Homo erectus*. The third gave rise to *Homo sapiens* and archaic society. The fourth saw the birth of history, including the births of agriculture, animal husbandry, the city, and the State (Morin, 1979). The fifth birth, possible although not as yet probable, would be the birth of humanity, which would end the Planetary Iron Age and the prehistory of the human spirit, and would civilize the Earth and witness a planetary community/society of individuals, tribes, and nations.

FROM ECONOMISTIC TO HUMAN DEVELOPMENT

The continuance of hominization must be seen as the unfolding of our potential, whether psychic, spiritual, ethical, cultural, or social.

We find here again the notion of development, but it has been much enlarged compared to the embryonic and mutilated idea that has been promoted and disseminated since 1950 or so (see Chapter 3) and that must be totally and radically rethought (development is in a developing crisis; see Morin, 1994). Development must be conceptualized anthropologically. True development is human development.

The notion of development therefore must be extracted from its economistic matrix. Development should no longer be equated with growth, which, as Jean-Marc Pelt has put it, "has become cancerous."[1] The notion of development must become multidimensional and escape from or break the Western molds that control its meaning and norms, not only the economic ones, but the cultural and civilizational ones as well. It must be divorced from progress, seen as a historical certainty, and redefine it as an uncertain possibility. It must involve the realization that nothing is obtained once and for all: Like all things alive and human, development is assailed by decay and must permanently regenerate itself.

DEVELOPMENT, CAPITALISM, SOCIALISM

It was believed that either socialism or capitalism were the true agents of development, with each being credited by its followers with a providential genius. Both brought about a recipe for economic order—with capitalism, the market and private ownership, and with socialism, the plan and State control—which would ensure social and human development. The so-called socialist formula, which in fact was totalitarian, has shown, besides being barbarous, that it was wont to aggravate the very problems it was bent on resolving, such as nationalist, ethnic, and religious enmities, and that its alleged democracy made difficult any democratic arrangements. Capitalism, for its part, has indeed procured the development of production, although through the use of barbarous methods, as noted by Marx, so that it cannot be seen as the sole or demiurgic key of human development. Similarly, the belief that the market has all the solutions to the civilizational problem is a reductionist, economistic error. The social advances of this century were obtained by the antagonistic/complementary action of bosses and workers' unions or parties within a democratic framework. As a matter of fact, Western societies cannot be defined only by the word *capitalist*: They are at once national, multicultural, democratic, pluralist, *and* capitalist.

In truth, development has been a myth, whether in socialist or capitalist form. Soviet style socialism is dying, and democratic socialism is exhausted. In its capitalist form, it enjoys only seeming health. For only a very short period it has looked like the magical formula to solve all problems.

---

[1]The French contains a pun between *croissance* [growth] and *excroissance* [tumor].

The notions of socialism and capitalism should not have providentialist, imperialist, and reductionist overtones. Rather, as far as capitalist economies are concerned, their power and creativity, their self-regulating and self-organizing qualities,[2] should be integrated into planetary civilization instead of the other way around. Anything strictly economical, like all that is strictly technological, is indeed as barbarous as it is civilizing and, for that reason, must be integrated into and subordinated to a politics of humanity. As to yearning after more community life and more freedom, which is what lies at the base of the word *socialism*, the politics of hominization must take this upon itself. That there be an end to the mutual exploitation of humans, which is also a socialist goal, must become a goal once again, although not by way of being a promise.

We should not ignore the fact that exploitation has bio-anthropological roots, namely, domination and enslavement, besides being deeply rooted in the very organization of historical societies, so deep that no political or economical change can ever really suppress it but only perhaps make it worse, as with totalitarian socialism. Therefore, although we will oppose for the moment the degrading forms of domination, enslavement, and exploitation, we must be wide open to the great aspirations of a humanizing process that is both far-reaching and long-lasting. We must be mindful that the worst aspects and tendencies of human beings and social relations never disappear and have to be continually controlled and checked, and better yet, check themselves.

DEVELOPING UNDERDEVELOPMENT AMONG DEVELOPED AND UNDERDEVELOPED COUNTRIES

As defined earlier, development involves simultaneously the unfolding of individual autonomies and the increase in communal participations, both neighborly as well as planetary. More freedom and more community, more self and less selfishness are essential.

Such an idea of development makes us aware of a key phenomenon in the Planetary Era: In developed countries, underdevelopment grows apace with techno-economical development.

The underdevelopment of developed countries is moral, psychological, and intellectual. To be sure, every civilization is more or less deprived, emotionally and mentally, and the human mind is everywhere seriously underdeveloped. However, what about the mental misery of wealthy societies, the want of love in sated

---

[2]For more on the market as spontaneous computer, see Morin (1990).

societies, the despicable nastiness and aggressiveness of the intelligentsia, the proliferation of empty general ideas and mutilated views, the loss of globality, depth, and responsibility? There is a misery that does not decrease with decreasing physiological and material misery, which rather increases with affluence and leisure. There is a specific development of mental underdevelopment under the primacy of rationalization, quantification, abstraction, irresponsibilization, which together instigate the development of moral underdevelopment.

Of course, there is more to our developing world, and a complex approach, open to ambivalence, allows us also to take into account the modern developments of individual autonomies, freedoms, communications, and the widened horizons brought about by travel and television, as well as the social securities and interdependencies, which, although implemented bureaucratically, make up for some injustices and alleviate some sufferings. We must not forget that bold, heretical, and deviant thoughts which, in traditional societies were destroyed in ovo, find in our world ways of expressing themselves. We must look at all the aspects of our situation and escape the euphoric/dysphoric double bind.

Rethinking development leads us to a critical rethinking of the equally underdeveloped idea of "underdevelopment." As we have seen, the idea of underdevelopment ignores the possible qualities and advantages of millenial cultures, which are—or were—part of so-called underdeveloped populations. It thereby plays a major role in dooming these cultures, which it considers as consisting of many superstitions. Arrogant alphabetization, which does not recognize the oral base of these cultures, but sees them as merely illiterate, only worsens the moral and mental underdevelopment of shanty towns.

There is certainly no point in idealizing cultures other than our own. Contrary to the view that every culture is in itself satisfactory, Maruyama (1992) makes the telling point that each culture contains aspects that are dysfunctional, misfunctional, underfunctional, and toxifunctional, operating imperfectly, misguidedly, ineffectually, and harmfully. Cultures ought to be respected, but in themselves they are as imperfect as we ourselves are. All cultures, including our own, are a hodge-podge of superstitions, fictions, obsessions, uncritically accumulated knowledge, glaring errors, and profound truths. Yet such a mix is not readily discernible, and one should be wary of classifying millenial knowledge as superstition, as, for instance, with the cooking of corn in Mexico. This practice was long attributed by anthropologists to magical beliefs, until it was discovered that it facilitated the body's assimilation of lysine, the nourishing substance in what was for a long time the Mexicans' only food. Thus, what seemed "irrational" was mere biological rationality.

Moreover, the notion of underdevelopment, admittedly barbarous, sets up an anthropological linkage between so-called developed and underdeveloped countries, giving rise to technical and medical assistance—drilling wells, finding new sources of energy, fighting endemic diseases and nutritional deficiencies—even within the context of economical exploitation, nature's degradation, and urbanization, all sources of new evils.[3]

Has not the very fight against poverty brought about new poverty, be it only because it wiped out sustenance economics or circulated currency where barter and mutual assistance had prevailed? Thus, by intending to develop, we did the opposite.

As long as we remain mentally underdeveloped, we will increase the underdevelopment of the underdeveloped. Lessening the mental poverty of the developed would rapidly, in our scientific era, procure solutions to the problem of underdeveloped material poverty. Unfortunately, we cannot manage to shake this mental underdevelopment. We are not even aware of it.

Therefore, we are driven to the view that mental, emotional, human underdevelopment, even of the developed, is henceforth a key issue of hominization.

METADEVELOPMENT

Development is indeed a goal, but we should stop making it a myopic or terminal goal. Development as a goal serves other purposes, namely, *true* living, *better* living. What does that mean? A living that includes understanding, fellowship, compassion, and that excludes exploitation, outrage, and contempt. That is, the goals of development are ascribable to ethical imperatives. The economy must be supervised and oriented by anthropo-ethical norms.

Continued hominization entails, then, an ethic of development, all the more so as the law of progress no longer offers any secure promise or absolute certainty.

As noted earlier, anything gained by humans, including gained development—or gains due to development—must incessantly be regenerated or else suffer losses. Recall all the historical backward

---

[3]This assistance could lead to the discovery of intermediary techniques, as proposed and imagined by Jean Gimpel, which would effect a transition between archaic techniques and more advanced ones.

movements and civilizational catastrophes dismissed by theorists of progress. It must be well understood to what extent the development of hominization is a risky adventure, a journey, an odyssey.

The consciousness of journeying spells insecurity and anxiety, as a result of destroying certainties, stability, and absoluteness, of giving up on happy endings. In this adventure, increased individualization brings about increased insecurity and anxiety. Similarly and consequently, we see neurotic/hysterical consumption and a thousand trivial pursuits in an attempt to quench the anxieties of individualization, except that this repression of anxiety only makes it worse, or else transforms it into aggressiveness.

In this way, we are led to a reform of thinking and a reform of life (to be discussed in Chapter 7). Should the idea of development include completely the adventure of hominization?

There is, among the goals mentioned, *true, better* living, the quest of something in excess of development. The significance of development goes beyond development; for instance, to develop an appreciation of music does not mean that the history of music is a progressive development, that Beethoven is better than Bach or Richard Strauss better than Beethoven. We must acknowledge the limitations of development as a concept, even when defined anthropologically, because the word suggests unfolding, unwinding, spreading. We must relate it dialectically to the idea of envelopment and involution, which brings us back to the origin or preworld, which immerses us in the depths of beingness and reimmerses us in antiquity, which involves reiteration, self-forgetfulness, a quasi foetal immersion in a beatific amniotic bath, a oneness with nature, reentry into myths, an aimless quest, a silent peace.

To be sure, Shelley, Novalis, Hoelderlin, Pushkin, Rimbaud, Bach, Mozart, Schubert, Beethoven, Moussorgski, and Berg are the historical products of civilizational development. Yet their works rise above this development and manifest our existence, tell us the unspeakable, bring us to the verge of ecstasy, to the point at which time and space loosen their unshakable hold. All that is essential in thinking punctures history, retroacts on the past all the way back to the point of origin, and carries us beyond the future.

Could not we then propose the notion of metadevelopment, meaning something beyond development, to which development (perhaps) would lead, and which it should not prevent?

THE PAST/PRESENT/FUTURE RELATION REDISCOVERED

Every society, every individual, exists by virtue of setting up a dialectical relation between past, present, and future, where each term supports the two others.

Traditional societies enjoyed their present and their future in obedience to the past. "Developing" societies obeyed, until recently, the future's commands while trying to preserve their past identity and to organize the present as best they could. Wealthy societies followed the dictates of both present and future, watching, first with glee but soon with melancholy, their past disappear.

The past/present/future relation, very differently implemented according to individuals and times, has now deteriorated almost everywhere in favor of a hypertrophic future. The crisis of the future brings about, in Western societies, an overemphasis on the present and a reactivation of the past. Here and there, ethnic and/or religious rerootedness, along with fundamentalism—the Islamic variety is only one among many—stem equally from the crisis of the future and the wretchedness of the present.

Almost everywhere, the living past/present/future relation hardens, atrophies, or jams. What we need then is a revitalization of this relation, respectful of each element, overemphasizing none.

The renewal and complexification of the past/present/future relation should consequently be recognized as one of the goals pursued by a politics of hominization.

Regeneration by the past can be obtained while and through being faithful to the two principles already stated. The first one acknowledges that all cultures have the right to exist, mindful that they have not achieved perfection. Each one entails specific inadequacies, blindness, deficiency, and their ability to promote individual existence is very unequal. Recall also that all particular cultures have acquired their uniqueness in contact with others through the appropriation of foreign elements, often typical of a conquering or conquered culture. Analogous to living species, all cultures have gone through changes and mutations, many of them becoming more complex through integrating what had been troubling or threatening to them.

Be this as it may, ethnic, national, and religious regeneration becomes backward as soon as it congeals in the direction of the past, loosening its ties with the present and the future.

The second principle of regeneration calls for a necessary reinvestment in the anthropological/biological/earthly ground, which is common to all humans and yet allows for particular regenerations.

The past means more than the particular past of an ethnic group or a nation; the tellurian, hominizing, and human past must also be appropriated and integrated.

The relation to the present, to life's enjoyments, should not be sacrificed to an authoritarian past or an illusory future. This relation now involves teleparticipation in the very life of the planet and the possibility of plugging into the circuits of the world's various cultures, as well as into the planetary culture and folklore itself. Besides, and most important, it is indeed in the present that life blossoms in a way that transcends development. The dialogically circular relation of the past/present/future restores the concrete thrill of being alive, which is at the heart of the present. As Saint Augustine said, there are three modes of time: past present, present present, future present.

Finally, the relation to the future will be revitalized to the extent that continuing hominization involves by itself an orientation toward the future. There is indeed no longer the illusory future of sure progress, but a risky and uncertain future, open to countless possibilities, in which human aspirations and purposes can be projected without, for that matter, any assurance of fulfillment. The restoration of a future so defined is for humanity supremely important and extremely urgent.

THE OUTWARD/INWARD RELATION

Human beings have always been polarized between two opposite callings. One of them, the extraverted, shows itself as curious about the outside world and has resulted in travel, exploration, and scientific research, including today cosmic exploration. The other, the introverted, is geared to the interior life, reflexion, meditation. From the onset of civilizations, astronomers turned skyward, and contemplatives turned their minds inward. There were technicians and mystics. It was also possible to change callings.

Today, the cosmic calling looms larger: to leave the Earth, to visit the other planets, and even beyond. To launch colonies in space presupposes terran unity and, even in the science-fiction hypothesis that Earth-born colonies would join in a grand confederation, our planet would all the more remain the primary homeland, the place where no artificial systems are needed, no oxygen tent, and no gigantic greenhouses.

The interior calling, long repressed and dismissed by Western society, is beginning to be heard once again: here and there, people are pulling away from activism, agitation, and distractions to achieve inner peace, a calm produced by spiritual training and not by drugs.

Management of the Earth does not entail abandoning the exploration of the material world and the prospect of a cosmic voyage, nor abandoning the inner quest. These two callings must continue—the one as well as the other on the Earth, the one as well as the other beyond the Earth.

THE CIVILIZING OF CIVILIZATION

The continuance of hominization, which would enable us to escape the planetary Iron Age, impels us to reform Western civilization—which has itself become planetary through spreading its woes as well as its wealth—so that the era of planetary citizenship might be established.

There is nothing harder to realize than the wish for a better civilization. The dream of personal development for all, of suppressed exploitation and domination in all forms, of real fellowship between all, of general happiness, has led its champions to the use of barbarous means that have ruined their civilizing enterprise. Every attempt at suppressing conflicts and disorders, at establishing harmony and transparency, ends up doing the opposite, with consequences both disastrous and manifest.[4] As is shown by the history of our century, the will to procure salvation on Earth has ended by building a hell. We must give up the dream of an earthly salvation. *To will a better world, which is our main goal, is not tantamount to willing the best of all worlds.*

A key problem—to be taken up later—is thus laid bare: Awesome obstacles stand in the way of civilizing civilization and jeopardize the very possibility of a civilizational politics.

CIVILIZING THROUGH DEMOCRACY

Democracy was born on the margins of history, on the side-lines of despotic empires, theocracies, tyrannies, aristocracies, and caste systems. It remains marginal, notwithstanding the universality of democratic longings. Yet it is the most civilized of political systems.

---

[4]Skepticism and nihilism ensue, acceptance of established order and disorder and the belief that inevitable injustices and mischiefs must lead us to accept serenely any oncoming evil. Such disillusionment obviously aggravates the difficulty of contemplating and undertaking any reform of civilization.

Modern democracy is the product of an uncertain history, within which, by fits and starts, its principles have appeared, have asserted themselves, and have evolved. The first of these principles, the sovereignty of the people, at once involved, precisely in view of buttressing this sovereignty, its self-limitation by the submission to laws and regulations as well as the periodic transfer of sovereignty to chosen representatives. Restricted at the beginning to the free men, it broadens its principle when all human beings are proclaimed to be born free and equal. National democracy follows urban democracy, but brings together hundreds of thousands or millions of citizens. This leads to the creation of parliament and separate powers, which were established to guarantee individual rights and to safeguard privacy. In 1789, the French Revolution established the democratic norm, supplemented in 1848 by the triune slogan: Liberty, Equality, Fraternity. This trinity is complex, as its terms are mutually complementary and antagonistic: left to itself, liberty kills equality and fraternity; compulsory equality kills liberty without achieving fraternity; and fraternity, without which no lived fellowship can possibly exist between citizens,[5] must check liberty and bring down inequalities, even though it cannot be promulgated or established by law and decree. Finally, socialism set out to democratize the economical/social organization of societies and not just the political.

It could appear that the principles were sufficient to define and defend democracy. Contemporary experience of totalitarianism was needed so that a fundamental aspect should be revealed, an aspect underrated, not to say hidden, until then—namely, democracy's vital connection to diversity and conflicts.

Democracy implies and enhances diversity among interests and social groups as well as diversity between ideas, which means that it should not impose majority dictatorship, but rather acknowledge the right to existence and to expression of dissenting minorities and allow the expression of heretical and deviant ideas. It needs a consensus on respecting democratic institutions and regulations, and it also needs conflicts between ideas and opinions in order to be alive and productive. However, vitality and productivity stem from conflicts only when democratic regulations are obeyed. The latter regulate antagonism by replacing physical with ideological battles and single out a temporary winner via debates and elections.

To the extent that it requires both consensus and conflicts, democracy is much more than the exercise of sovereignty by the people. It is a complex system of political organization and

---

[5]See Morin (1990), in which the point is made that, sociologically speaking, there is growth in complexity if there is fraternity.

civilization that nurtures (and is nurtured by) the inner autonomy of individuals, their freedom of opinion and expression, as well as the triune ideal of Liberty, Equality, Fraternity.

In order to take shape and set down roots, this system requires conditions that are also complex. Democracy depends on conditions that depend on its own exercise (the civic spirit, acquiescence in the democratic rule), thus its frailty.

No wonder, then, that it is so difficult to establish democracy in the wake of the totalitarian experience. The democratic rule requires a political and civic culture that decades of totalitarianism in Eastern Europe have impeded; the economic crisis stirs up conflicts in excess of what the democratic rule can possibly tolerate, whereas nationalist exasperations pave the way for the dictatorship of an impassioned majority over peaceful minorities.

Even the West has to cope with serious democratic problems, not only because the democratization of its democracies is not yet finalized and entails inefficiencies or deficiencies, but also because democratic regressive processes have become visible within them.

First, technobureaucratic development brings about the domination of experts in all fields that, until then, had been answerable to political discussions and decisions. Nuclear technology, for instance, leaves citizens, representatives, even ministers, out of every decision concerning the use of nuclear weapons. As far as developing locally this new energy resource, decisions are made more often than not without seeking the advice of citizens.

Technoscience has invaded territories left until then to biology and sociology, such as fatherhood, motherhood, birth, and death: It is already possible to produce a child whose father is unknown or even dead, to achieve conception without pregnancy, as it is already possible to diagnose—and eliminate—an abnormal fetus. It will soon be possible to have the fetus conform to parental wishes and social norms. These issues have not entered the political consciousness nor the democratic debate, except for the right to abortion. Worse still, the widening gap between an esoteric, hyperspecialized technoscience and the knowledge available to citizens sets apart those who know—albeit their knowledge is piecemeal and unable to contextualize and globalize—and those who do not know, that is, citizens as a whole. We are thus led to the necessary task of democratizing knowledge, in other words, to a cognitive democracy. This task may seem either absurd to technocrats and scientocrats or impossible to the citizens themselves, and it certainly cannot be undertaken except by way of popularizing scientific knowledge beyond the student age and university precincts,[6] or, more importantly, by way of reforming thinking so as to allow for a coming together of the various sciences.

At the same time, heightened economic competition between nations, especially when business is in a slump, fosters a reduction of the political order due to the fact that its permanent agenda is economical. Ideas and ideologies being also in crisis, the acknowledged primacy of the economy brings about a soft consensus that weakens the role, necessary to democratic life, played by the conflict of ideas.

Furthermore, democracy regresses socially: Up to the early 1970s, progress and growth helped level out inequalities, but afterward economic competition and the pursuit of productivity cut out a growing number of workers, while proletarians and immigrants live in ghettos that set them apart from the still climbing portion of the population. The econocrats, so good at adapting people to technical progress and so poor at the reverse, cannot invent new solutions for reorganizing work or distributing wealth. In this way, a "dualist" society is established, which, if the democratic deficit persists, will then become the norm.

Connected with this, the collapse of great hopes for the future, the deep crisis affecting revolutionism, the exhaustion of reformism, the flattening of ideas within everyday pragmatism, the inability to formulate a great design, conflicts of ideas losing ground to conflicts of interests or racism and ethnocentrism, all foster the sclerosis of parties and weaken participation, which in itself is fostered by this sclerosis and weakening.

In this democratic regression, the great civilizational problems that we indicated earlier are still being seen as private issues instead of being publicly debated. Such is the multifarious way that the key problem of democratic deficiency is raised for Western societies—that is, the need to renew democracy, whereas everywhere else in the world it is a question of its implementation. The democratic problem is planetary and multifarious. Generalized democratic longing collides with generalized democratic difficulty. Democracy is conditioned by civilization, which is conditioned by democracy.

We meet again with our contradictory purposes. It is imperative that we stand up to the forces that threaten democracy, that we preserve what these forces would destroy, as well as that we choose to foster democracy's progress, in other words, that we set it among the major goals of hominization.

---

[6]In France, the creation by and in the *Centre National de la Recherche Scientifique* (CNRS) of a center *Sciences et citoyens* [Science and the citizen] is a start in that direction.

EARTH FEDERATION

The civilizing of civilization involves intercommunication between societies, and beyond this their organic association on a planetary scale. This goal becomes unquestionable as soon as, on all continents, the nation has exhausted its historic function of freeing colonized or subjected populations and when it shows itself in turn to be capable of subjugating minorities.

Should we do away with the nation-state? We have noted already that it stands for a sizable anthropohistorical power: the power of the Mother-/Fatherland myth, a religious power (the nation divinized and worshiped), and the organizational power of the modern state. The failure of international socialist associations in the 20th century, the weakness of globalism, and the toilsome formation of Europe evince the power vested in the multifaceted reality of the nation-state. Today, the generalized national claim laid by countless ethnic groups agrees undoubtedly with the legitimate recognition of sovereignties as well as disagrees with necessary evolution.

Besides, to reiterate, if the nation-state has become powerful enough to destroy masses of people and societies, it has become too small to look after great planetary problems, and too big to look after the concrete individual problems of its citizens. The change of scale brought about by developing economic globalization has de facto rendered the powers of the nation-state outdated. Furthermore, the nation-state is unable to protect cultural identities which, being provincial, act in self-defense, precisely by asking for state power to be curtailed.

Going beyond the nation-state should involve a reduction of state bureaucracy, a beneficent outcome considering that "every state has to treat free human beings like mechanical cog-wheels".[7]

This does not amount to doing away with the nation-state, but rather involves inserting it within more extensive associations and restricting its absolute life and death power over ethnic groups and individuals (in this regard, political interference is conceivable), without abridging its competence over issues that it can handle at its own level (subsidiary principle).

---

[7]From the so-called German Idealists' program, attributed to Hoelderlin, Schelling, and Hegel (see Krell, 1985).

Going beyond the nation-state in favor of more extensive associations will become a fact of life, and hence effective, only if Europeans credit Europe with a matripatriotic quality, if Africans, Latino-americans, and so on do similarly, and if all credit Earth with being motherland and fatherland to us all.

In any case, a planetary association is rationally and minimally required by a contracted and interdependent world. We must consider, as implied by this association, a planetary citizenship that would give and guarantee terran rights to all. Such an idea appears as utopian today, and yet Caracalla's edict of 212 realized it by granting Roman citizenship to all the inhabitants of an empire that, in his own eyes, was equal to the world itself.

A new geopolitics is called for, one not built around the interests of nations and empires, but one off-center and subject to associative dictates, one capable of setting up cooperative linkages between zones rather than strategic and economic zones of influence. This politics will be implemented only if many approaches are made to converge.

The United Nations should be at the center of these decentralizations. It should also be a planetary police force, coming into action when a state attacks another state, a population, or an ethnic group, until such a time when it could rely on democratic forces throughout the world strong enough to restore democracy wherever it would be overthrown. The formation of new planetary institutions, connected to the UN, should also be furthered, together with the elaboration of joint programs targeting vital issues, as, for instance, in Rio 1992. Transnational, international, and metanational associative structures of every sort should be considered, drawing from the historical experiments made by the hanseatic cities, by the Holy Germanic Roman Empire, and by the Roman Empire, not with the intent of repeating them, but of stimulating creative futurology with their examples in mind.

In order to materialize these possibilities, we would need, as Jean-Marie Pelt has put it, "a planetary public opinion." We would need a planetary citizenship, a planetary civic consciousness, a planetary intellectual and scientific opinion, and a planetary political opinion. These opinions have not even begun to be formulated. Yet, they are preliminary to a planetary politics, which in turn is prerequisite to the formation of these opinions and realizations.

The human association of which we dream should in no way "be grounded on the hegemonic model of the white, adult, technical, and Western male; it should rather betoken and awaken feminine, youthful, elderly, multi-ethnic, and multi-cultural civilizational ferments" (Morin & Piattelli-Palmarini, 1974).

The idea would be to move toward a universal society based on the genius of diversity (homogeneity lacks genius), which would lead us to a double imperative, inwardly contradictory but fruitful for that very reason: (a) everywhere to safeguard, propagate, cultivate, or develop unity; and (b) and everywhere to safeguard, propagate, cultivate, or develop diversity.

We thus have the following paradox: Cultures must be simultaneously preserved and opened up. There is nothing new in this. At the origin of all cultures, including the most bizarre, we find encounters, unions, syncretisms, and cross-breedings. All cultures have the ability to assimilate what had been foreign, to a certain extent at least, measured by their vitality, beyond which they become assimilated by what is foreign or/and disintegrate.

Thus, according to a twofold complex dictate, harboring a contradiction that we cannot conceal (but can we leave it behind? Is it not required by the very life of culture?), we must simultaneously protect cultural specificities and promote cross-fertilizations and cross-breedings: We need to tie together the preservation of specificities and the propagation of a mestizo or cosmopolitan universality, which leads to the destruction of these specificities.

Can integration not disintegrate? For archaic cultures, the Inuit being a case in point, the problem is tragic. There should be ways to have them benefit from the advantages of our civilization (e.g., health technology, comfort, etc.) and ways to help them preserve their traditional lore (e.g., medicine, Shamanism, hunters' know-how, knowledge about nature, etc.). We need middlemen, the likes of Jean Malaurie, who would have nothing in common with missionaries, either religious or lay persons, come to shame them out of their beliefs and habits.

Recall that cross-breeding has always created new diversity while it fostered intercommunication. Alexander the Great used to marry a few hundred indigenous girls to his Macedonian soldiers in each conquered city of Asia, and these cities, traversed or founded by him, became the matrix of brilliant Hellenenistic civilizations and the source of Greco-Buddhist metis art. Roman civilization itself became rapidly cross-bred because it assimilated the Greek inheritance: It included in its pantheon a great number of foreign gods, and, on its territory, barbarous populations became Roman by right while preserving their ethnic identity.

Artistic creativity feeds on influences and confluences. Thus, flamenco, which today looks most authentic and original, is in fact similar to the Andalusian people itself, the end result of Arabic, Jewish, and Spanish interpenetrations, transformed in and by the sorrowful genius of gypsies. We can hear and see in flamenco the fruitfulness and dangers of the twofold imperative: preserve (the origin), and open (to the foreign). With regard to preservation, there have been, first, thanks particularly to the *aficion* of a few French amateurs, the study and rediscovery of the *cante jondo*, which had become substantially debased. Thus old records were revived in *recopilaciones*, forgotten and fallen performers became masters all over again and taught, in line with tradition, new generations of performers now fully regenerated. With regard to evolution, there has been, first, a degenerate mishmash of Spanish tunes purportedly from Sevilla, then an upgrading of sources in the music of Albeniz and De Falla, and finally interesting and recent cross-breedings with outside sounds and rhythms, such as jazz (Paco de Lucia playing with John MacLaughlin) or rock (the best of Gipsy Kings).

Jazz began as an Afro-American cross-breed, a unique product of New Orleans, which then spread throughout the United States, spawning many varieties and allowing the old styles to maintain themselves alongside the new ones. It became a music Blacks and Whites listened to, which both danced to and performed. In all its forms, jazz spread throughout the world. The old New Orleans style came back to life in the cellars of Saint-Germain-des-Prés, went back to the United States, and took up its abode again in New Orleans. Next, combined with rhythm and blues, rock music arose in American White culture, and from there spread throughout the whole world, taking on all languages and national characters. Today, in Beijing, Canton, Tokyo, Paris, and Moscow, people dance, celebrate, and come together through rock, and youth of all countries glide along together to a planetary rhythm.

The worldwide spread of rock has called forth new cross-bred inventions, such as rai, brewing up the rhythmic broth of rock fusion, within which the musical cultures of the whole world espouse one another. In this way, sometimes for worse, but also often for better, and all along not being divested of themselves, musical cultures of the whole world inseminate one another, although remaining unaware of their planetary offsprings.

It follows that people and cultures must be allowed to preserve a generalized and diversified cross-breeding, which in turn is itself a cause of diversity. Taboos and curses which, in the era of the human diaspora, functioned as the immunological defense of archaic cultures and dogmatic religions, have become obstacles to communication, to mutual understanding, and to creativity in the Planetary Era. Those who mix up styles are at first held to cause confusion; ethnic and religious cross-breeds are repudiated by their original communities as bastards and heretics. However, they are victims and martyrs in a pioneering process of understanding and love.

The great civilizing areas of mediterranean Antiquity and Islam, also the great modern empires, had witnessed the flowering of cosmopolitan metropolises such as Alexandria, Rome, Baghdad, Cordova, Istanbul, and Vienna. Next, modern nationalism, burning for unity, expelled diversity in the countries that had belonged to the Ottoman Empire, for instance, Lebanon and Algeria, and expelled it in Yugoslavia and in the former Soviet Union. Another process had started, however, in the Americas—granted that irretrievable cultural destructions had come before. New cosmopolitan cities grew up, such as New York, San Francisco, Los Angeles, and Sao Paolo. Large mestizo populations have become the majority in Brazil, Mexico, and Venezuela, giving rise to original cultures. Without yet intermingling, entertaining in fact still many prejudices, Whites, Blacks, Chicanos, and Amerindians live together in the United States, with a great number having the same ambitions and life styles. Simultaneously, small-scale civilizations continue being annihilated—for instance, that of the Amazon Indians—and what survivors get from colluding with Whites is not cross-breeding but catastrophic disintegration.

We will become watchful and aware of cultural legacies, as well as aware of the need to regenerate them, on the condition that we truly become citizens of the world, that is, cosmopolitan.

That is why we designate ourselves as being cosmopolitan, which means, etymologically, citizen of the world, and concretely, child of the Earth—and not a rootless abstract individual. We wish for networks to grow within the planetary fabric; we call for cross-breeding, when it is a symbiosis and not when a civilization takes advantage of another one.

The terran identity card of the new citizen of the world involves a group of concentric identities: family, city, province, and nation. Western identity, even when it will have possessed itself of elements stemming from other civilizations, will have to be seen as only one facet of earthly identity.

Internationalism aims for the human species to be one people. Globalism wants it to be one state. What matters is to turn the human species into humanity and the planet Earth into a common home for human diversity. A planetary society/community would truly achieve human unity/diversity.

YES BUT . . .

Yes, these are fine ideas, and fine words, but do they have any chance of being carried out in a world which, as we have seen in the preceding chapters, is plunged in turmoil and unable to change?

5

Impossible Realism

AN UNCERTAIN REALITY

Realism can have two meanings in politics. The first requires that we not struggle against reality, that we adapt to it; the second requires that we take stock of reality in the hopes of transforming it. Yet there are multiple uncertainties regarding the reality of what is called reality.

To begin with, we could say that reality is that which is immediate. Yet this immediacy itself refers to two different realities: the one temporal, the other factual.

The first has to do with the reality of the present. This reality is quite strong and has abolished a part of yesterday's reality, but it is also very weak, as it will itself be partially abolished by the reality of tomorrow. History has no end of illustrations of the fragility of realities that seemed obvious and triumphant in their own todays. Thus, from June 1940 to October 1941, the domination of Hitler's Germany over all of Europe was the crushing reality. The Wehrmacht, throughout the summer of 1941, reached the Caucasus, the gates of Moscow and Leningrad, whose fall seemed certain. A conquered France had become vassal to Germany. A marginalized

England sought shelter from German bombs. The United States kept out of the war. Realism seemed to dictate adaptation to the ineluctable reality: submission to the conqueror.

In the summer of 1940, however, De Gaulle saw another reality: Whereas for most the war was already over, for him it had just begun. He believed that the great powers not involved in the war—the U.S.S.R. and the United States—would eventually become so. He foresaw that the war would encompass the whole world and that the superior forces that would engage themselves in it would overcome the Third Reich. To be sure, this reality, which took effect in 1942-1945, was not predetermined.

What would have happened if the German offensive had not been delayed on June 21, 1941, following the coup of the preceding month in Belgrade, which forced Hitler to lose a few weeks liquidating the Yugoslav army? And what if the Russian Winter had not arrived so early and been so brutal, immobilizing the Wehrmacht's transports and allowing Moscow and Leningrad not to fall? What if the Japanese had not dragged the United States into the war through the bombing of Pearl Harbor in December 1941? It was, in any case, by no means inevitable that Nazi Germany would collapse. It might have established a durable hegemony in Europe. In periods of crisis and war, reality is turbulent, with unforeseeable bifurcations and upsets.

However, realism was not where it seemed to be—on the side of the immediate triumph of force. It was not unrealistic to believe in the defeat of that force. One must sometimes know how to wager, beyond realism and irrealism.

The factual meaning of the term *reality* refers to situations, facts, and events that are visible in the present. Yet perceptible facts and events often hide facts or events that go unperceived and can even hide a still invisible reality. Beneath the crust of visible reality there is a subterranean and occult reality that will emerge later but that remains completely invisible to the realist. There are Sphinx-like events, whose messages cannot really be decoded until they have become realized. The nomination of Gorbachev as secretary general of the Soviet Communist Party is a small Sphinx-like event that became enormous. It was unrealistic in 1988 to foresee the rapid collapse of the gigantic empire. It was, however, realistic to think that the totalitarian system was being undermined by problems that it had managed to overcome until that point (see Morin 1981, 1983, 1984, 1990). Yet it was in no way realistic to foresee the self-destruction of the U.S.S.R. in 1992.

Once again, we come across zones of uncertainty in the make-up of reality, zones that strike the various realisms with uncertainty, and sometimes reveal that what seemed unrealistic was in fact realistic.

I would add that there are many realities that are very difficult to grasp—this is also true, and especially so, for the experts—as is the case, for example, with the global economic situation: Is it a matter of the provisional coincidence of localized depressions, or symptoms that presage a grave global crisis?

This shows us that one must know how to interpret reality to be able to recognize what is realistic. This also shows us to what extent the meaning of situations, facts, and events is dependent on interpretation.

All knowledge, as well as all perception, is an act of translation and reconstruction (see Morin, 1985), that is, interpretation. The reality of anything taken as a whole can only manifest itself through theories, interpretations, and systems of thinking. All knowledge of political, economic, social, or cultural reality is embedded in systems of interpretation of the nature of politics, the economy, society, and culture, which in turn are interdependent with respect to a system of interpretation of the nature of history.

It is these systems that can lend to abstract conceptions, imaginary perceptions, and mutilated visions or ideas, a quasi-hallucinatory appearance of reality for those who believe in them.

The Bolsheviks believed they knew the reality of history and society: Imperialism, capitalism, class conflicts, the historical mission of the proletariat, and the necessary advent of the classless society were examples of the many dogmas furnished and confirmed by their system of interpretation for the nature of situations, facts, and events. The adventure of communism believed it was firmly on the path of historical reality. It was, in fact, a rebellion against historical reality.

The economistic interpretation of reality forgets about the role of noneconomic structures and phenomena. It ignores accidents, individuals, passions, and human folly. It believes it is grasping the deeper nature of reality by means of a conception that binds it to the complex nature of this reality.

Recognition of the complexity of reality—of our human, social, and historical reality—is no simple matter. The paradigm (see Morin, 1991) of disjunction/reduction, which controls most of our modes of thinking, separates the different aspects of reality from one another and isolates objects or phenomena from their environments. It is incapable of integrating the transformative potential of time and thus remains closed to the possible.

This is why all knowledge of reality that is not animated and controlled by the paradigm of complexity is bound to be mutilated and, in this sense, to be lacking in realism.

However, the paradigm of complexity, which assists us in recognizing the complexity of realities, does not provide certainty. On the contrary, it helps us reveal not only the uncertainties inherent in the very structures of our knowledge, but also the black holes of uncertainty in the realities of the present. Thus, reality does not merely consist of what is immediate. Reality is not clearly visible in the facts. Ideas and theories do not reflect reality—they translate it, and in a manner that can be mistaken. Our reality is nothing other than our idea of reality. Reality, too, is something of a wager.

So, given the difficulty of recognizing reality, we might ask: Is it realistic to be realistic? The stunted realism that thinks reality is self-evident and can only see the immediate is in fact blind. In the words of Bernard Groethuysen: "To be realistic, how utopian!"[1]

THE DIALECTIC OF THE IDEAL AND THE REAL

We come now to another problem: Do ideas hold a certain power over reality, which would mean that they have a reality and a power of their own?

As I (1991) discussed elsewhere, ideas and myths take on reality. They impose themselves on people's minds and can even impose themselves on historical reality and, through violence, change its course.

The October Revolution of 1917, dictated to Lenin by the idea that he had to deliver socialism from the belly of history, in fact gave birth to totalitarianism.

As the following course of events demonstrated, reality does not spontaneously or immediately reject the idea that contradicts it. There are ideas charged with terrific energy: so it is with all great ideas and all great beliefs. In the struggle between the ideal and the real, the latter is not always the stronger (Morin, 1991). Ideas can acquire a terrifying strength through drinking the blood of the real.

The ideal subsumed the real in the U.S.S.R. It annihilated anything that opposed it from within by destroying the peasantry in this land of peasants. It muzzled reality and forced it into hiding. It erected an immense totalitarian reality with the greatest military power of all time. However, the triumphant idea began to degrade in its very triumph. A new reality took shape, born of the marriage of the idea and the old reality, and shaped totalitarianism in its modern form—having become, for more than half a century now, a major reality in the history of the world. This increasingly vigorous totalitarianism was neither capable of conforming itself to socialist

---

[1]Personal communication.

aspirations nor of acquiring the economic efficiency of capitalism. Then came the idea of reforming reality. This idea, at the summit of its power, opened itself to the doubt, self-questionings, and disillusionment of a few leaders to become the new political idea. Yet this idea did not know how to handle the reality that the totalitarian framework had mastered, and the thaw of that reality led to its collapse.

There is a relation of uncertainty between the ideal and the real. The ideal can impose itself on the real, but the latter will not thereby conform itself to the ideal. The offspring produced by the copulation of the ideal and real often bear no resemblance to either of the parents.

One could imagine a politics generated from the dialectic between *idealpolitik* and *realpolitik* (Korber, 1990), but again we meet with the uncertainty of reality and thus of the realism of *realpolitik*. We risk ending up with either the pious wishes and blindness of ideal and idealistic politics, or with the acceptance of all established order and every accomplished fact.

What is possible? If there are insufficient constraints to allow for the predetermination of history, there are constraints that prohibit certain possibilities. It is a question of knowing which constraints are constraining.

There are some constraints that appear absolutely constraining, but that harbor their own breach. Thus the constraints of physico-chemical organization made impossible the emergence of living beings until the latter appeared in a deviant fashion with the emergence of new principles of organization. Similarly, the appearance of human language was impossible before the complex anatomical/genetic/sociological/cultural revolution that allowed for the repositioning of the skull and the formation of a supralaryngeal cavity, where, with the softening of the vocal cords and the evolution of the palate, sounds came to be articulated. Before the existence of agriculture and cities, very strong constraints—the dispersion of small, hunter-gatherer societies without a state—prevented the organization of agriculture and cities.

Which constraints are, for us, insurmountable? The only universally insurmountable constraint is the second principle of thermodynamics that does not allow for perpetual motion, immortality, or an earthly paradise.

Insurmountable sociological and economic constraints within a given system can, however, eventually be overcome through and in a metasystem, as was the case of living systems with regard to physicochemical systems, or of human language with regard to the call system, or of historical societies with regard to archaic societies. Metasystems obviously have their own constraints. There are no systems without constraints. The impossibility of doing away with constraints tells us that there is no best of worlds, but this does not prohibit the possibility of a better world.

Thus, we return to uncertainty; not only the uncertainty attendant on the arrival, as sudden as it is frequent, of the unexpected, the accidental, and the new (Gorbachev, Yugoslavia, etc.), but also a more profound uncertainty respecting social and human possibilities.

THE WAGER

The principle of the ecology of action (see Morin, 1990), which extends into the principle of political ecology, refers to the fact that an action tends to break away from the intention (idea) of those who initiated it as soon as it enters the play of inter-retro-actions of the environment into which it is introduced. Thus, the "aristocratic reaction"—which led to the convening of the Estates General of 1789, in which, thanks to the class system, the nobility thought to regain privileges that had been taken away under absolute monarchy—ended up having the opposite effect of liquidating all privileges of the aristocratic class.

The revolutionary uprisings of 1936 in Spain, by contrast, provoked the reactionary Franquist coup. Just as in meteorology a small bifurcation in a critical zone can lead to an enormous chain reaction—the so-called "butterfly effect"[2]—so a few slight modifications in the thinking of the leader of the immense totalitarian empire will unleash a reform that, although initially prudent and local in scope, will become generalized and amplified. In a volatile mixture of actions and reactions, the failure of the conservative reaction triggers the explosion, which leads, in just two years, to the collapse of the empire itself. History, too, has its "butterfly effects."

In any case, the long-term consequences of any political action are totally unforeseeable at the start. The series of consequences following the events of 1789 were unexpected. The terror was unforeseen, as were the Thermidor, the Consulat, the Empire, the reinstatement of the Bourbons, and so on. In a broader sense, the European and global consequences of the French

---

[2]The beating of a butterfly's wings in Australia can trigger a tornado in New York.

Revolution, up to and including October 1917, were unforeseen, as were the consequences of October 1917, from "socialism in a single country" to the rise and fall of a totalitarian empire.

All of this reflects the fact that political reality is subject not only to the uncertainty of reality that we have considered earlier, but also to the effects of the uncertainty principle of the ecology of action.

The classic problem of ends and means should itself be set within a relation of uncertainty. Ignoble means employed toward a noble end cannot only contaminate this end, but also become ends in themselves. Thus, the Tcheka, designated to eliminate counter-revolutionaries, not only contaminated the socialist project, but also became an end in itself throughout its successive incarnations as the Guepou, the NKVD, and the KGB—a supreme, self-perpetuating policing force.

The ecology of action tells us at the same time that good intentions can lead to detestable effects and that bad intentions can produce excellent effects, at least in the short term (as, for example, what happened when the failure of the Moscow putsch of 1991 made possible the abolition of the dictatorship of the Communist Party). We must equally, therefore, dialectize the problem of ends and means, that is, refuse to grant to either term a sure dominance over the other (see Morin, 1981).

The ecology of action would seem to invite inaction, and this for the following reasons: (a) the perverse effect (the unexpected harmful effect is more important than the hoped-for beneficial effect); (b) the futility of innovation (the more things change, the more they stay the same); and (c) the threat to acquired gains (we want the better society, but we manage only to suppress liberties and securities). We must certainly take into account these three considerations, which were validated in a terrifying manner with the Bolshevik revolution and its aftermath. However, they do not have the value of deterministic certainty, lack of innovation, and, moreover, can give free rein to decomposing, degrading, and despoiling processes and, for this reason, be fatal.

The ecology of action, therefore, does not invite inaction, but a wager that is aware of its risks and a strategy that allows for the modification, even the cancellation, of the action undertaken. The ecology of action calls for a dialectic of the ideal and the real.

THE POSSIBLE/IMPOSSIBLE

It is possible today, both technologically and materially, to reduce inequalities, feed the starving, distribute resources, slow down population growth, diminish ecological degradation, change the nature of work, create various high authorities for planetary regulation and protection, and develop the U.N. into a veritable Society of Nations to civilize the Earth. It is rationally possible to build a common house, to cultivate a common garden. Communications and information technologies would make it easier to pilot our planet of 3 billion human inhabitants than was the case with the France of Louis XIV with its 20 million inhabitants.

There is the possibility of a planetary public opinion: Through the media, there are flashes of planetary solidarity with Rumanian orphans, Cambodian refugees, and Bosnians in distress. There are conscious flashes of terrestrial citizenship.

The possibilities for the coming to consciousness of our common destiny increase along with the perils. These possibilities are nourished by the Damoclean threat of nuclear arms, the degradation of the biosphere, and the degradation, equally global, of the anthroposphere through heroin and AIDS.

As we have seen, planetary union is the minimum rational requirement for a shrinking and interdependent world. Yet this possible union seems impossible with the necessity of so many transformations in mental, social, economic, and national structures.

Thus, the possible is impossible. We live in an impossible world where it is impossible to achieve the possible solution.

Yet, the possible/impossible is realistic, in the sense that the word *realism* signifies that it corresponds to real possibilities in the economy, agriculture, technology, science, and so on. *Yet it is this planetary realism that, at present, is utopian!*

THE ENORMITY OF CONTRARY FORCES

To civilize the Earth, we must be conscious of the very problem of civilization. Civilization is but a thin crust on the surface of our being and our societies. We must reinforce the crust, but this presupposes a profound transformation of human relations, which is precisely the problem.

There is a barbarism in civilization, not only in the sense of Walter Benjamin (1970), for whom all civilizations are born of barbarism, but in the complex Freudian sense (repression, the non-annihilation of barbarism by civilization) as well as in the modern organizational sense (the combined developments in science, technology, and bureaucracy that create a specific kind of civilizational barbarism).

No amount of good wishes and projects will suffice. It would take so many simultaneous and convergent reforms that it hardly seems possible, given the enormity of contrary forces.

THE IMPOSSIBLY POSSIBLE?

Are we not falling back on the hopes of Buddhists, Christians, and socialists, which, until now, have always failed us? Complex thinking, conscious of ambivalence, of the bad in the good, of the good in the bad, of impossible perfection, of the impossible achievement, of the ecology of action, of the ever unexpected overlapping of inter-retro-actions, of the impossible liquidation of the "negative," is thereby conscious of the enormous difficulty.

It would take fantastic human progress to resolve the most elementary of problems. Admit that the situation is logically hopeless: the more change becomes necessary, the more multidimensional and radical it becomes; the more multidimensional and radical, the more our mental, social, and economic systems make it impossible.

Yet if the situation is logically hopeless, this indicates that we have arrived at a logical threshold at which the need for change and the thrust toward complexification can allow for the transformations that could bring metasystems into being. It is when a situation is logically impossible that novelty and creativity, which always transcend logic, can arise. Thus, it is when the chemical organization of groups of millions of molecules became impossible that a living auto-eco-organization first appeared.

To be sure, and I have already said as much, ethically and politically necessary progress is not a historical necessity. Progress itself is affected by a principle of uncertainty. What we hope should be the avant-garde of a historical planetary movement is and might turn out to be nothing more than a small rear guard of resistance against barbarism. Here again we find the imperative of resistance discussed previously (see Chapter 4).

We are not ineluctably condemned. The forces of barbarism, fragmentation, blindness, and destruction that make a planetary politics utopian are so threatening for present-day humanity that they indicate *a contrario* that the politics of hominization and planetary revolution answer to a vital need.

I am not pronouncing any "oughts" dictated by the idea! Marx said: "It is not sufficient that the ideal go over to the real. The real must also go over to the ideal." There is, at present, this double movement: Real globalizing forces are moving in the direction of the ideal, and ideas can take on reality by highlighting the planetary import of fellowship and mutual comprehension for the collective forces running through this century. Unfortunately, there is also a movement within the real that runs in the opposite direction. Here again we happen on uncertainty. However, if the uncertainty of the real is fundamental, then the *true realism* is that which, while taking local certainties into account along with the probabilities and improbabilities, *grounds itself in the uncertainty of the real*.

The uncertainty of the mind and that of the real offer both risks and opportunities. The insufficiency of immediate realism opens the door to what lies beyond the immediate. The problem is to be neither realistic in the trivial sense (to adapt to the immediate), nor unrealistic in the trivial sense (to exclude oneself from the constraints of reality), but to be realistic in a complex sense (to comprehend the uncertainty of reality, to know that there are possibilities still invisible in the real), which often seems unrealistic. Here again, reality eludes the realists and utopians alike.

Global reality cannot be fully grasped. It includes enormous uncertainties due to its complexity, its fluctuations, its mixed and antagonistic dynamisms, its impossible-seeming possibilities, and its possible-seeming impossibilities. The ungraspability of global reality retroacts on the singular parts because the becoming of the parts depends on that of the whole.

We are, then, faced with the unheard of paradox in which realism becomes utopian and the possible becomes impossible. However, this paradox also tells us that there is a realistic utopia, and that there is a possible impossible. The principle of the uncertainty of reality is an opening in both realism and the impossible. It is through this opening that we must introduce anthropolitics.

As we have already seen: To go beyond realism and irrealism, one must know how to wager.

6

Anthropolitics

FROM POLITICS TO ANTHROPOLITICS

During this century we have moved from good government politics to providence politics, from a laissez-faire state to a welfare state.

Politics first took the economy under its wing with 19th century protectionism and later with antitrust legislation. Then it took charge of the economy through steering and stimulating its growth, through state control or even public offers of contracts, and through overall planning.

The needs of individuals and populations have entered the sphere of political jurisdiction. For example, personal security is obtained by an array of allowances—life, work, sickness, old age insurances—as well as services—maternity, day nurseries, homes for the aged, funeral homes. The reparation of damages caused by natural disasters (floods, earthquakes, etc.) is increasingly listed among the tasks of governments. The educational politics of governments has become systematic and has been enlarged to encompass culture and leisure. The freedom or control of modern media is a political issue. More generally, prosperity and well-being have acquired the status of political goals.

In this manner, politics has penetrated all the pores of society, and all the problems of society have penetrated it in turn.

Issues of living and surviving, defined literally in a biological sense, have burst into politics in a spectacular and generalized way. Health care politics has replaced public relief, concerning itself with the whole population and not only with the sick and crippled. It has taken charge of the struggle against cancer and AIDS as much as against drugs and even tobacco. A politics of guaranteed minimum living wage has become widespread among wealthy countries, whereas, in poor countries, the struggle against starvation has fallen within the competence of international politics. Demography has become a major political concern, whether the trend be toward depopulation or overpopulation.

Possible biomedical interventions that now alter and transform death, birth, and identity, raise political problems. For example, euthanasia, the extraction of organs, blood transfusion, the right to abortion, the conservation of sperm, artificial conception, mothers bearing children not their own, and most of all genetic engineering that will make it possible to choose the sex, the physical traits, and maybe even the psychological makeup of the expected child, have become issues larger than individuals and families, requiring political decisions.

Thus, with the transmitting mechanism of heredity and the inherited patrimony itself possibly being modified, human nature and human sociability become political issues: Life, birth, and death lie henceforth in the political arena. The notions of father, mother, child, masculine, and feminine, in other words the pillars of the family and of society, are altered by these disturbances and require political norms. The idea of a human being, now at the mercy of engineers, runs the risk of being rapidly standardized by a political power capable of controlling the controllers.

Faced with fundamental anthropological problems, politics is becoming unwillingly and often unwittingly *anthropolitics*—a politics of humanity.

At the same time, the planet as such becomes political while politics becomes planetary: The threat to humankind of nuclear weaponry had already been a major political problem. For about 20 years now, ecology has become not only a local political problem (degradations of ecosystems), but also a global one (changes in the biosphere).

Thus, politics must deal with the many facets of human problems. Because development has become a major political goal and the word *development* means assuming—in an admittedly subconscious and mutilated way—political responsibility for human becoming, politics is also, in ways equally subconscious and mutilated, responsible for humanity's becoming in the world. Human becoming in the world now involves the philosophical issue, henceforth political, of the meaning of life, of human goals and destiny. *Practically, then, politics is led to assume responsibility for the destiny and becoming of humanity, as well as that of the planet.*

TOTAL AND TOTALITARIAN POLITICS

Dating from the French Revolution, a providentialist mythology and a quasi-religion of salvation had burst into, then spread through, politics. According to Saint-Just, revolution would bring happiness to Europe. Marx, for his part, transformed 19th-century socialism into a religion of earthly salvation, whose proletarian messiah would put an end to anything oppressive or divisive among humans. Compared to the social democrats' assist/protect understanding of the providential function of politics, this providence took up an almost religious this-worldly-salvational significance in its Marxist-Leninist form. Thus, politics was vested with the great mission of the religions of salvation, except that, instead of offering salvation in heaven after death, it promised it on Earth during one's lifetime.

The idea of a revolution that would change the world and change life, vivified by a powerful myth and a ruthless will, has prompted a totalitarian politics, which stamped the 19th century with its awesome religious and mythical unfolding. Its apex and eventually its collapse have shown that if politics can weigh on all aspects of social life, it can neither tackle nor solve all human problems.

Yet, in its own providentialist and religious way, totalitarianism has expressed the contemporary features of politics, according to which politics relates to all aspects of human life and assumes responsibility for the future of humankind in the world.

POLITICS DRAINED AND FRAGMENTED

As it inflated to the point of becoming totalitarian, traditional, nontotalitarian politics was drained and fragmented. The economy, technology, medicine, biology, and so on have entered into politics, introducing within state and party councils and structures, econocrats, technocrats, bureaucrats, experts, and specialists who have fragmented jurisdictions on the basis of compartmentalized disciplines and thought patterns.

Then, in a growing number of countries, where old ideological feuds have subsided, politics has been drained of great ideas in favor of economic goals (e.g., stable currency, rate of growth, external trade balance, productivity of firms, competitiveness on the international market), so much so that, in the present phase, politics is conducted, not to say swallowed, by the economy.

So we find ourselves in the midst of a draining and sclerosis of traditional politics, incapable of fathoming the new problems which appeal to it; in the midst of a politics that encompasses multi-faceted issues, handling them in compartmentalized, disjointed, and additive ways; and in the midst of a debased politics that lets itself be swallowed by experts, managers, technocrats, econocrats, and so on.

Hence, there is great difficulty: A politics of humanity must take on itself all human problems in their totality, without becoming totalitarian. It must embody management, technology, and the economy, without being dissolved and depolitisized by management, technology, and the economy.

Multidimensional politics should address very diverse and specific problems, although not in a compartmentalized and fragmented fashion. This requires technicity and scientificity, but a politics of humanity should not submit to systematic specialization and ignore globality, ultimacy, and responsibility. On the contrary, it must unceasingly promote the vision of what is global (planetary), the apprehension of what is ultimate (the meaning of life, human goals), and a sense of responsibility, which is consequent to consciously shouldering ultimate and global problems.

Finally, if it is true that the imaginal is more than some insubstantial mist and belongs to the complex stuff of human reality, if it is true that myth is not a mere superstructure but one of the elements—produced and productive, causing and caused, in the self-organizing process of culture and society—if it is true that affection, love, and hatred are not ascribable only to private contingency, but make up an essential part of what is human, then politics is not allowed to envisage issues only at the prosaic level of what is technological, economic, or quantitative.

The poetic promise to "change life" having collapsed, politics has become hyperprosaic (technicized, bureaucratized, and econocratized). We should know, though, that humankind dwells on Earth both poetically and prosaically (as will be discussed in Chapter 8[1]), and that poetry is not a mere variety of literature, but a lifestyle involving participation, love, earnestness, communion, enthusiasm,

---

[1]We will expand on Hoelderlin's phrase: " . . . poetically, man dwells on this Earth" (Hamburger, 1980, p. 601).

ritual, feast, ecstasy, dance, and singing, whereby prosaic life, which is made of practical, utilitarian, and technical tasks, is effectively transfigured. There is a necessary complementarity or alternation between prose and poetry.

It follows that, if it should no longer dream of doing away with the prose of the world as part of its endeavor to bring happiness on Earth, neither should the politics of humanity shut itself in the prosaity of "postindustrial society" or of "technical progress."

Politics, which indeed permeates multiple human dimensions, is not humanity's sovereign. The reduction of all these dimensions to the political dimension can only be a mutilating and pretotalitarian reduction. *Nothing evades politics, but each politicized object remains out of politics one way or another.* Politics encompasses everything but stands to be encompassed by the whole that it encompasses. The point is to tie politics and these human dimensions together dialectically. When admitted into politics, anything human must have an anthropological stamp. The idea, then, of anthropolitics (the politics of humanity; Morin 1969) should not reduce to itself all the dimensions it encompasses: It must develop political awareness and political specificity, while acknowledging and respecting what, in them, eludes politics.

The idea of a politics of humanity leads to the idea of planetary politics, just as the idea of planetary politics leads to the idea of a politics of humanity. Both concepts relay the fact that politics should no longer be, only or mainly, the politics of ethnic groups, parties, and states.

The manysided, planetary, and anthropological feature of politics results from a basic awareness: *what lay at the borders of politics (the meaning of human life, development, the life and death of individuals, the life and death of humankind) becomes the nucleus. It is then up to us to devise a politics of humanity in the world, a politics of planetary responsibility, a manysided but not totalitarian politics. The development of human beings, of their mutual relations, of social life, is the very program of the politics of humanity in the world, a call for ongoing hominization.* A politics of this nature goes beyond *aggiornamenti* ("updatings"), modernizations, and postmodernizations, even though, as discussed later, it does not neglect at all what is immediate, local, regional, and short range.

ANTHROPOLOGICAL COMPLEXITY

Any politics aiming at human development and at a better world must of necessity ask the question: What should we hope for? This leads us to wonder about humanity, society, and the world.

Marx did just that and undertook an extensive and serious inquiry, following the scientific principles and philosophical categories of his day. Unfortunately, he deemed permanent what was only a step in the development of science; he convinced himself ingenuously that he had discovered the Law of History—but history is a gypsy and, like love, *n'a jamais connu de loi* (has never been bound by laws). He satisfied himself with a truncated and promethean humanity, oblivious of imaginal humanity and of the other side of *Homo sapiens*, namely, *Homo demens*. He accompanied his belief in progress with an unconscious messianic strenuousness that included faith in a political messiah (the proletariat), in an apocalypse (the revolution), and salvation (a classless society). Today, as we have seen, the fifth century of the Planetary Era has the physical, biological, and social sciences that certainly do not amount to exhaustive anthropo-bio-cosmological knowledge, but at least acknowledge the complexity of *sapiens demens*, the complexity of life, the complexity of the Earth, and cosmic complexity. Today, in spite of strong opposition from mental and institutional structures, complex thinking is taking its first steps and, without mixing up or fusing everything, endeavors to connect that which was separate while preserving distinctiveness and differences.

Complex anthropology can enlighten anthropolitics. Humanity has not been commissioned to exert absolute power over nature. However, further hominization is open to it—a risky business indeed, with *Homo sapiens demens* having both original goodness and original vice tightly intertwined (see Morin, 1979). This ambivalence must be taken in stride. It involves weaknesses, miseries, deficiencies, mercilessness, goodness, nobleness, possibilities of destruction and creation, consciousness and unconsciousness.

COMPLEXITY AT THE HELM: POLITICAL ECOLOGY AND THE ROLE OF STRATEGY

Recall the principle of political ecology. Politics does not reign over society and nature; it unfolds autonomously/dependently (see Morin, 1990) within a social ecosystem, and the consequences of its actions, at once caught in the web of social and natural inter-retro-actions, answer only briefly and seldomly to the intent or will of the actors. This is even more true in the Planetary Era, when generalized interdependence makes it so that local and particular actions have general, far-reaching, and unexpected consequences. The ecological principle of political action must therefore be unceasingly present in anthropolitical thought and planetary politics.

Strategy is the rational guidance of an action in a situation and context that is ill defined and perhaps dangerous. Strategies are elaborated according to goals and principles, consider various possible scripts for the unfolding action, and select the one that appears to be dictated by the situation. Sometimes the preferable script is that which lowers the risks as well as the opportunities, and sometimes it is that which heightens the opportunities, as well as the risks. Strategies change the script along the way according to the information, reactions, hazards, events, and the unexpected appearance or disappearance of obstacles, growing richer in experience as well as in ability to combat adversity.

The strategy of planetary anthropolitics is doomed to unfold in a thoroughly ill-defined context. Twenty-five years ago, futurologists made forecasts that deluded us momentarily, but that have since collapsed. There are so many processes clashing with each other, conflicting, interdependent, and hazardous, so many chain interactions and retroactions that no assured future is predictable. We can only wager that the future will be as we wish, a possible although uncertain future, when we devise the strategy that precisely dovetails with the planetary condition.

The strategy of planetary anthropolitics must be elaborated under the beacon and guidance of the goals highlighted earlier (see Chapter 4).

Anthropolitical principles are complex, inwardly uncertain, and/or conflicting. Such, for instance, is the case with the principle of the ecology of action. This principle is inwardly uncertain but allows for the action to be corrected or dropped whenever it goes against the original intention. We have already indicated that dialogical principles involve two or three complementary/antagonistic dictates, such as the principle that links together in the following manner:

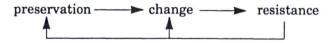

preservation ⟶ change ⟶ resistance

The dialogical principle that must link together transformation and regulation must also be recognized. Any transformation both disorganizes and reorganizes, as it destroys old structures in order to make new ones. Any innovative transformation is deviant and, because preestablished regulations foreclose deviancy, it must break these rules as well as establish new ones in order to prevent the disorders that would foreclose the innovation itself. Principles, norms, and rules are thus needed in order to dissolve the rules that preclude innovation and to establish the rules that stabilize transformation.

We have already hinted at the principle of "minimax," according to which heightened opportunities involve heightened risks and, conversely, lowered risks involve lowered opportunities. In the first case, the choice is bold; in the second case, it is prudent. It is difficult to know for sure when prudence should be preferred to boldness. As far as the evolution of our planet in general is concerned, we have already suggested, when we counted deceleration among our Earth-centered goals, that prudence must become a global principle. However, this global principle does not mean at all that acceleration should not be necessary at critical junctures, or that boldness should not be called on in order to jostle inertia. Similarly, we must promote the moral principle according to which means should agree with ends, but a complex understanding of the ends-means loop has shown us that, in limited cases, "bad" means alone can save us from the worst.

There is also the principle of complementarity between the principles of solidarity and globality, which demands that we handle at a planetary level problems of global and general interest, and that of subsidiarity, which grants national, regional, or local echelons the right to handle autonomously problems that fall within their jurisdictions.

Recall finally the peculiar complexity of the triune principle: Liberty, Equality, Fraternity. As much as they are complementary— a minimum of freedom and of equality is required for fraternity, and a minimum of fraternity to prevent freedom from being licentious and equality from being denied even in principle—these words are also mutually antagonistic because freedom threatens equality and ignores fraternity, equality requires strictures offensive to freedom, and fraternity, unlike the two other principles, cannot be imposed or guaranteed by any law or Constitution. Nonetheless, Jean Onimus has said that fraternity is more utopian than liberty or equality because even these will never be completely established. Having said this, we must refer again to the principle of the ecology of action in order to make sure that the virtues of liberty, equality, and fraternity will not be corrupted. How many crimes against freedom have been perpetrated in the name of freedom, against equality in the name of equality, against fraternity in the name of fraternity?

Anthropolitical strategy must also obey norms, by which is not meant moralizing precepts, but rather rules of conduct that emerge from confronting principles, goals, and ideals with facts, current arguments, and unfolding evolutive tendencies. In short, norms depend simultaneously on goals, principles, and on an empirical assessment of the conditions of action. Thus, the prudence principle and the quality principle—"less but better"—can be seen as norms. The following two permanent norms can be singled out.

Norm I: To work at what unites, to fight against what separates.

It does not follow that hegemonic coercion should be maintained over nations and ethnic groups wishing to liberate themselves, but it does follow that, in that very instance, liberation should be conducive to necessary participations in associative wholes and not to isolation and ruptures of preexisting economic and cultural connections. Thus, for instance, the liberation of the Baltic Countries should go hand in hand with their integration in a new Baltic superstructure—including Sweden, Norway, Finland, Denmark, Russia—and the settlement of special links with Russia, not only in view of safeguarding economical complementarity, but also in view of providing a protected status to Russian minorities.

More generally and more deeply, agreement, that is, associative fellowship, must become, in the words of Arturo Montes, the new prime mover of history, to which would be subordinated the other traditional mover, namely, struggle.

Norm 2: To target concrete universality.

What stands in the way is not only due to ego- or ethnocentric elements that always sacrifice the general interest to particular interests, but also to a seeming universality, that supposedly knows and serves the general interest, although it is in fact led by an abstract rationality. The norm of the concrete universal is very difficult to apply. The general interest is neither the sum total nor the negation of particular interests. The ecology of action teaches us that action serving the general interest may be diverted in a particular direction. Our notion of general interest should often be reexamined with reference to our concrete universe, which is the planet Earth.

The strategy of complex politics requires the awareness of interactions between areas and issues, so as not to handle them piecemeal. It must avoid onesided or crude handlings. As an analogy, take the example of crops protected against a pathogenic agent. Pesticides, of course, destroy pathogenic agents but also other useful species. They interfere with ecological controls based on interactions between antagonistic species and foster the harmful overpopulation of certain species. They impregnate grains and vegetables, thus adulterating the quality of food. Alternatively, an ecological intervention aimed at destroying or weakening a noxious species may be made by introducing a species that is an antagonist of the pathogenic agent and by looking out for possible chain reactions.

Politics has not moved beyond solutions of the pesticide type; it tackles isolated factors instead of taking into account looped interactions. Thus, concerning health, demographic, lifestyle, and environment issues, we hold to separate policies and do not have a politics dealing with interactions between these problems.

Furthermore, we should not attend only to the mainstreams but be mindful that any prevailing current brings about countercurrents that eventually become very powerful. Such was the case with the neoarchaisms, neonaturisms, neonaturalisms, and neoregionalisms that emerged in opposition to the great homogenizing and urbanizing current of the 1960s. So it was with the ecological current that astonished and stunned industrial and urban policies (Paillard, 1981), beginning during the early 1970s.

THREE KINDS OF TIME

Political strategy must operate simultaneously on many levels and face ceaseless ranking problems. The motorist who wants to get somewhere the fastest and/or quietest way must in the first place skirt the blocked road, escape from a traffic jam, and dodge the uncautious pedestrian. Meanwhile, he or she must pay attention to what lies ahead, up to the limit of their visual field, anticipate a possible traffic jam, be ready eventually to change route, and, if needs be, enter a prohibited route, against the rule of the road. Similarly, political strategy must ceaselessly coordinate the immediate, middle, and long terms.

The perspective changes from one to the other term, and yet no real borderline separates them, as they rather overlap and present the one to the other. These three terms must be attended to at the same time, which means that the middle and long terms must be present in the present term.

The Immediate or Present Term

Politics must function on a day-to-day basis, all the more so as the future is blurred. We navigate at sight, sometimes blindly.

Immediate-term politics deals with emergencies, as well as with long-term preparations. The emergency situation requires a pragmatic attitude and a lesser evil policy; it also requires an inversion of principles. As affirmed by Hippocrates and Avicenna, we must treat the causes of a disease and not the symptoms, which calls for a deep and long-term cure. Yet, when the sick are at death's door, symptoms must be attended to—first of all the fever—before undertaking any deeper treatment. It happens, however, that repeated emergency interventions lead to an abandonment of deeper treatments, and myopic, day-to-day politics becomes the norm instead of remaining the exception.

The immediate is more and more jostled by so many urgent demands made on the protection of life—local wars that threaten to become general, atomic dangers, brutal flares of barbarism, natural and/or technical catastrophes. The immediate pressures give rise incessantly to a double bind between deep political exigencies, involving intellectual and material investments that only show returns in due time and advantages, gains, or pleasures of the hour.

The notion of the present or short term, as somewhat wider than the immediate, sets up a connection between the immediate and middle terms. It calls for *aggiornamento* and political organization, in view of doing away with the old and going ahead with the indispensable adaptation to the needs of the present. Whereas it may be necessary to give up methods, recipes, and formulae, it may be advisable to make sure in the first place that they are such indeed and that they are not just old-fashioned, since old-fashioned objects are often more sturdy and lasting than fashionable ones. We should not model ourselves in politics on those Breton peasants, who installed white wood, factorymade pieces of furniture in place of their old, hardwood, hand-crafted ones, given or sold to the secondhand dealer, only to discover later and too late how valuable they were.

Should we rely on—and plan for—today, even though we are moving beyond it? In the matter of education, for instance, "modernism" thinks that we must adapt the university to the present social needs of the market and of the economy, whereas the university's task is also to insert into the present the centuries-old traditions that it carries. On the contrary, it is in the present that, in spite of academic resistance, a reform of thought must be initiated, without which we could not rise to the complex challenge leveled at us by reality. Such a reform would be much more than an *aggiornamento* and modernization, as it would cater to the needs of ongoing hominization.

People think that we must adjust ourselves to the present, when in fact adaptation must be reciprocal between us and the present. Modernization ought to be banned if, by this word, one intended to advocate an acceptance of what is modern as a natural necessity and to involve an adaptation of politics to what is given. Politics, on the contrary, must be modernized by adjusting to the new anthropological and planetary problems that have arisen within the political sphere. However, modernity must also be politicized by precisely including it in the anthropological and planetary perspective.

In this sense, we must do better than *aggiornamenti,* modernizations, myopic and superficial postmodernisms. Politics must at once adjust to the present and adjust the present to itself.

The Middle Term

Middle-term politics is one that goes along with Earth-centered goals, playing the part of a mediator that takes into account difficulties, resistances, currents, and countercurrents. The principles and norms of anthropological strategy spelled out previously must assert themselves in the middle term.

The Long Term

Long-term politics yields to the attraction of the goals contemplated earlier, and key ideas and ideals should constantly be recalled.

As with the middle term—and more so—the long term demands, in the very present, a political and philosophical investment, although one totally overlooked by those who herald a better world. To invest in political rethinking involves a veritable refoundation, which requires that thinking itself be reformed.

THREE ZONES OF SPACE

The microphysical universe, the macrocosmic universe, and the mesophysical universe of our median zone, lying between the infinitely great and the infinitely small, are dissimilar in nature, notwithstanding the fact that one and the same universe is at stake. Similarly, the microsociological universe (of relationships between persons), the mesosociological universe (of ethnic groups and societies), and the macrosociological universe (of extensive civilizational areas and planetary space) are dissimilar, even though one and the same universe is at issue. Politics usually functions at the mesosociological level. It has a tendency to forget about person-to-person, or microrelations (that is, concrete individual lives), and about the concrete universal of planetary issues. It is incumbent on anthropolitics to take these three zones into account and to supply the zone-specific principles and strategies of hominization.

Finally, keep in mind what characterizes the planetary era in the 20th century, namely, the making of a complex, planetarized space-time, in which all societies, carried along by the same currents of time, experience their own different times, whether archaic, rural, industrial, postindustrial, and so on. All this must lead us to break with the idea that all societies should henceforth align themselves with the fastest time, our clock time, or with Western time. We should rather be led to experience the complementarity of different times, to stem the tide of clock time, to decelerate Western time.

PREPARING THE DECELERATION

Our civilization is inflicted with "speeditis." It is urgent that we become aware that the race is mad and can get out of hand. We must brake and slow down in search of a new rhythm. It is henceforth imperative to consider an international control of growth and economical competition and to enact a charter of life norms, including the rights of human time.

How best to slow down? This problem requires a global awareness identical to the one that first began to appear at the Earth Summit of Rio. It is a problem that, in an era of interdependence, cannot be handled by any single nation, except at the price of an asphyxiating self-sufficiency.

The leading industrial powers, however, could take the initiative and start the deceleration. Thus, the United States' decision, dictated in part by the ecological lobby, not to commercialize the supersonic plane has prevented its worldwide spread. For the first time in the 20th century, a technical solution through increased speed has not been accepted; it has at least been postponed. Norms of unclocked time might be considered in many human activities, along with a return to remuneration linked to the work performed, to the finished object, or to the service rendered, and not to the time spent working. We might rehabilitate slowness—*lentum in umbra*—in daily life, widen and increase convivial opportunities, in which a truly human time is to be found, and extend the sabbatical year to all professions. Finally, the new technologies, which allow increased production while saving human energy, invite us today to reconsider the notion of work—which is less and less geared to energy and more and more to information—and to find a remedy for overspecialization and reverse the domination of clock time and the rigid logic of artificial machines.

PREPARING FOR THE METATECHNICAL ERA

The third technological revolution (the steam engine was the first, electricity the second) is computational/informational/communicational in nature. Its tendency is to alleviate the burden of distance and space. Networks predominate over localizations—telex-fax-radio-computer networks already undergird world trade—and work can more and more dissociate itself from a central place.

Technological progress will soon make it possible to envision a new logic for artificial machines, a natural logic closer to that of the brain, thanks to the fabrication of quasi-neuronal networks of computers, capable of changing work itself and not only life outside of work.

Consequently, there is hope that technology will stop being the blind guide of our future; it has become thinkable to insert technology among human goals. We must then prepare for the metatechnical era.

Thus, we see that the strategy of a planetary anthropolitics at once requires that conflicting purposes be maintained, that very different demands timewise and spacewise be fitted together as best they can, and that resources for rethinking, verification, and modification be constantly available.

To be sure, any strategy is an art, and artfulness appears not so much in the application of rules—of the art—as in the alternative or polyphonic use of rules. Saint-Just had an intimation of this when he stated that, to date, the art of government had only produced monsters.

Having materialized, having become a movement and a tendency, anthropolitics will need many centuries to reach its goals, if it reaches them at all. Even if ever achieved, the task will have to be performed over and over again.

7

The Reform in Thinking

There is a profound blindness regarding the very nature of what ought to constitute relevant knowledge. According to the ruling dogma, relevance increases with specialization and abstraction. However, a minimum of knowledge about knowledge teaches us that the most important factor is contextualization. Claude Bastien (1992) notes that "cognitive evolution does not proceed through the setting up of increasingly abstract ways of knowing, but, on the contrary, through the setting of these ways in their proper contexts." It is this contextualization which determines the conditions of applicability and the limits of validity of the knowledge in question. Bastien adds: "Contextualization is an essential condition for efficiency (of cognitive functioning)."

Specialized knowledge is itself a particular form of abstraction. Specialization abs-tracts, that is, it extracts an object from a given field, rejects the links and interconnections with its environment, and inserts it in the abstract conceptual zone of the compartmentalized discipline, whose boundaries arbitrarily break the systemicity (the relation of a part to the whole) and the multidimensionality of phenomena. It leads to mathematical abstraction that splits itself off from the concrete, in part by favoring everything that is calculable and formalizable and for the rest by ignoring the context necessary for the intelligibility of its objects.

Thus, economics, which is the most advanced of the social sciences in terms of mathematics, is the most socially and humanly backward of the sciences, as it abstracts itself from the social, historical, political, psychological, and ecological conditions that are inseparable from economic activities. This is why its experts are less and less able to interpret the causes and consequences of monetary and stock exchange perturbations, and to foresee and predict the flow of the economy, even in the short term. Therefore, economic incompetence becomes a major problem of the economy.

Knowledge must certainly make use of abstraction, but it must do so in seeking to construct itself with reference to context and, in so doing, mobilize what the knower knows about the world. As François Recanati (1992) puts it: "Comprehension of the facts, far from reducing itself to a plain and simple act of decoding, is a non-modular process of interpretation which mobilizes general intelligence and appeals in a general fashion to one's knowledge of the world" (pg. 21). What this means is that the comprehension of particular facts can only be relevant when one engages and cultivates one's general intelligence and mobilizes one's overall knowledge in each particular case. As Marcel Mauss used to say: "One must recompose the whole." I add to this: One must mobilize the whole. To be sure, it is impossible to know everything about the world or to grasp its multiform transformations. However, although chance-ridden and difficult to attain, one must strive for knowledge of key information concerning the world, otherwise one will be condemned to cognitive imbecility. This is true even more so given that the current context of all political, economic, anthropological, ecological, and so on, knowledge is the world itself. The Planetary Era demands that we situate everything in the planetary context. Knowledge of the world *as* world has become an intellectual as well as a vital necessity. It is the universal problem of every citizen: how to gain access to global information, and how to acquire the possibility of linking together and organizing it. To do so, and thereby recognize, acknowledge, and know the problems of the world, we need a reform in thinking.

FRAGMENTED THINKING

Thinking that compartmentalizes, divides, and isolates allows the specialists and experts to be very effective in their compartments and to cooperate efficiently in noncomplex areas of knowledge, especially those having to do with the functioning of artificial machines. However, the logic that they obey extends to society and human relations the constraints and inhuman mechanisms of the artificial machine, and their deterministic, mechanistic, quantitative, and formalistic vision obscures or dissolves everything that is subjective, affective, free, and creative. What is more, fragmented and technobureaucratized minds are blind to inter-retro-actions and circular causality, and they often regard phenomena from the perspective of linear causality. They perceive living and social realities according to the mechanistic/deterministic conception, which is only valid for artificial machines. More largely and profoundly, the technobureaucratic mind is as incapable of perceiving as of conceiving the global, the fundamental, and the complexity of human problems.

Problems are spatially and temporally interdependent, whereas disciplinary research isolates problems from one another. There is, to be sure, especially in the matters of the environment and development, an initial rise in consciousness conducive to the promotion of interdisciplinary research. Yet despite an affectation of important gains to this effect, the results are meager because the degrees, carriers, and systems of evaluation take place within the disciplinary framework. There is, above all, a resistance on the part of the mandarin/university establishment to transdisciplinary thinking equal to that of the Sorbonne of the 17th century relative to the development of the sciences.

The possibility of thinking and the right to think are denied by the very disciplinary organization of scientific knowledge and by the closing in of philosophy on itself. Most philosophers scorn devoting their reflections to new knowledge that modifies conceptions of the world, reality, humanity, and so on. For the first time in the tradition that began with the Greeks, they have their backs to the cosmos, to the destiny of humanity in the world, to the aporias of reality. The world is struggling for its life, while they discuss the sexuality of Oedipus, debate a *Lebenswelt* with neither *Leben* nor *Welt,* and ignore the reform in thinking to the profit of reforms in spelling.

Scientists deny to nonscientists the aptitude, right, and ability to think about their discoveries and theories. What, then, of the writings of Einstein, Heisenberg, Bohr, Monod, Jacob, Prigogine, Reeves, d'Espagnat, and Hawking, to name a few? If they wrote books for nonscientists, it is because they considered that their ideas could be readily understood. To be sure, technical or mathematical competence is not possessed by the "average person," but such ideas can be communicated and discussed in a language common to us all. Behind the equations of quantum physics, there is the idea that the world of the microphysical does not obey the same logic, structures, and laws of our mesophysical world, even though our world is constituted on the basis of this microphysical texture. Behind Boltzmann's equation of the second principle of thermodynamics, there are ideas on the degradation of energy, the disorganization of systems, and the role of disorder in the physical world that concern each and everyone of us.

FALSE RATIONALITY

In our own times, the potentially ill-fated effects that the conjunction of experts, commissions, and administrations exert on decision making can lead, in the end, to tragedy. Such was the case with the affair of contaminated blood. To be sure, all unexpected and surprising information naturally runs counter to received opinion and to the habitual ways of thinking that such information perturbs. It risks, moreover, being chloroformed indefinitely by office routine or of being dispersed and rejected at the hands of hyperspecialized organizations that fragment whatever problem with which they have to deal. These organizations, supported by the irresponsibility of commissions, dissolve the sense of responsibility. Warnings and alerts are often repeated without success and succeed only too late at overcoming inertia and blindness, and it takes a disaster before countermeasures are finally organized.

It even happens that immediately beneficial measures, once subjected to a compartmentalized and linear mindset, produce harmful long-term effects that counterbalance, and even surpass, the beneficial ones. Thus, the Green Revolution, promoted to nourish the Third World, brought about a considerable increase in food resources and, most notably, allowed for the avoidance of scarcity. However, it became necessary to rethink the initial idea that, although apparently rational, sought an abstract maximization of returns—to select and multiply the most quantitatively productive vegetable genome over vast stretches of land. It was then realized that the absence of genetic variety allowed the pathogenic agent, against which this genome had no resistance, to wipe out an entire crop in the same season. One then had to reestablish a certain genetic variety so as to optimize, rather than maximize, the yield.

At the same time, massive use of fertilizers impoverishes the soil. Irrigations that ignore the lay of the land lead to an equal impoverishment. The accumulation of pesticides destroy interspecific regulations, eliminate useful species along with the harmful ones, and even sometimes lead to the unexpected multiplication of a harmful species that have become immune to pesticides; toxic substances contained in the pesticides then make their way into foods that alter the health of consumers.

Finally, clear-cut logging over thousands of hectares (1 hectares = 100 acres) contributes to the imbalance of water levels and growing desertification. The great monocultures eliminate small, subsistence polycultures and aggravate scarcity, which causes a rural exodus and the swelling of urban shantytowns.

Everywhere on the planet, as François Garczynski puts it, "this kind of agriculture makes deserts, in the dual sense of term: soil erosion and rural exodus." For example, if not regulated, blind deforestation, along with the destruction of trees outside the forests, will transform the tropical sources of the Nile into dry wadi for three quarters of the year. Imprisoned by the logic of unbridled production, the capitalists, politicians, and technicians responsible for Amazonian deforestation in the interests of agriculture, the raising of livestock, and industry want to ignore the fact that the recycling of cloud moisture by the forests furnishes half the outflow of the Amazon. By the same token, most agronomists still do not understand the vital role of isolated trees that control the flow of water, air, and chemical elements in the soil, work to purify both water and air, and act as conservers of fertility (Garczynski).

False rationality, that is, abstract and unidimensional rationalization, triumphs over the land. Hasty regroupings, furrows too deep and longitudinal, unchecked deforestation, the paving of roads, urbanization that looks only to the profitability of land surfaces, and pseudofunctional planning that ignores needs that cannot be quantified through questionnaires, contribute to the increase of low-rent suburbs and new cities that rapidly become islands of boredom, filth, degradation, negligence, depersonalization, and delinquency.

The victims and consequences of resulting human catastrophes are, of course, left out of the accounts, along with the worsening of natural catastrophes, as in the recent case of Vaison-la Romaine in France (where an overflow of the Ouzève river flooded suddenly and mercilessly a new district of the city).

Everywhere, and for decades now, supposedly rational solutions, put forward by experts convinced that they were working for reason and progress, and that the customs and fears of the populations they encountered were based on mere superstition, have impoverished as much as they have enriched and have destroyed as much as they have created. The most monumental masterpieces of this technobureaucratic rationality were realized in the U.S.S.R.: Rivers were diverted to irrigate, even during the hottest times, hectares of treeless land to cultivate cotton, which led to the salinization of the soil through the surfacing of mineral salts, the evaporation of underground water, and the drying up of the Aral sea. The damages were greater in the U.S.S.R. than in the West due to the fact that, in the U.S.S.R., the technobureaucrats did not have to deal with the reactions of citizens, who, in their eyes, were so many ignoramuses and mental incompetents. Unfortunately, after the collapse of the empire, the directors of the "new states" called on the experts from the liberal thinking West, who deliberately ignored the fact that a competitive market economy needs appropriate institutions, laws, and rules. Wavering between, on the one hand, a piecemeal economic reform, incapable of bringing about the required structural transformation, and on the other, an immediate and generalized liberalization that would trigger sociological degradation, the new directors have not worked out that indispensable complex strategy that, as Maurice Allais has already noted (although himself a liberal economist), calls for a plan for the abolition of plans and a program for deprogramming.

Intelligence that is fragmented, compartmentalized, mechanistic, disjunctive, and reductionistic breaks the complexity of the world into disjointed pieces, splits up problems, separates that which is linked together, and renders unidimensional the multidimensional. It is an intelligence that is at once myopic, color-blind, and without perspective; more often than not it ends up blind. It nips in the bud all opportunities for comprehension and reflection, eliminating at the same time all chances for a corrective judgment or a long-term view. Thus, the more problems become multidimensional, the less chance there is to grasp their multidimensionality. The more things reach crisis proportions, the less chance there is to grasp the crisis. The more problems become planetary, the more unthinkable they become. Incapable of seeing the planetary context in all its complexity, blind intelligence fosters unconsciousness and irresponsibility. It has become a bearer of death.

One aspect of the planetary problem is that intellectual solutions, whether scientific or philosophical, to which we habitually appeal, are themselves the most urgent problems and the ones most difficult to resolve. As Aurelio Peccei and Daisaku Ikado have put it: "The reductionist approach, which consists in relying on a single series of factors to regulate the totality of problems associated with the multiform crisis we are currently in the middle of, is less a solution than the problem itself."

Mutilated thinking that considers itself expert and blind intelligence that considers itself rational are still the order of the day.

FROM RATIONALIZATION TO RATIONALITY

Mutilated thinking and blind intelligence claim and believe themselves to be rational. In fact, the rationalist model that guides them is mechanical, deterministic, and excludes all contradiction as absurdity. This model is not rational, but rationalizing.

True rationality is open and enters into dialogue with a reality that resists it. It shuttles incessantly between the logical and the empirical. It is the fruit of the considered debate of ideas and not the property of a system of ideas. A reason that ignores living beings, subjectivity, emotions, and life is irrational. One must make room for myth, feeling, love, and regret, and consider them rationally. True rationality knows the limits of logic, of determinism and mechanism; it knows that the human mind is not omniscient and recognizes the mystery of reality. It negotiates with the irrationalized, the obscure, and the irrationalizable. It must struggle against rationalization that, although both draw from the same sources, merely encloses fragments of reality in its would-be exhaustively coherent system. True rationality is not merely critical, but self-critical. It is recognizable in its ability to recognize its own insufficiencies.

Rationality is not a property, whether understood as the quality with which certain minds are gifted—scientists and technicians, for instance—and which others lack, or the virtue of which technicians and scientists are the proprietors.

We must awaken from the illusion, so dear to the West, that we are the sole proprietors of rationality and must break the habit of judging cultures according to their technological performance. Along with its myths, magic, and religion, every society manifests rationality in the making of tools, hunting tactics, and the knowledge of plants, animals, and the land generally. In our modern societies, similarly, there is a persistence of myth, magic, and religion, including a providentialist myth cloaked beneath the idea of reason, as well as a myth of progress. A true and full rationality, for its part, must break with providentialist reason and the rationalizing idea of guaranteed progress. Only then is it free to consider, in all its complexity, the earthly identity of human being.

THINKING IN CONTEXT

It is impossible to conceive of our earthly identity and of anthropolitics without a thinking capable of relinking disjointed notions and compartmentalized areas of knowledge. The new scientific discoveries capable of revealing Homeland Earth—the

Earth as system, the biosphere, the place of the Earth in the cosmos—have no meaning as long as they remain separated from one another. To repeat, the Earth is not equivalent to the addition of a physical planet, plus the biosphere, plus humanity. The Earth is a complex biological/anthropological totality wherein life emerges out of the history of the Earth and humanity emerges out of the history of terrestrial life. The relation of humanity to nature must not be conceived in a reductionistic or disjointed manner. Humanity is a planetary and biospheric entity. Humans are both natural and supranatural beings that, although rooted in living and physical nature, emerge from this nature and distinguish themselves from it through culture, thought, and consciousness/conscience.

Fractured thinking, which cuts up everything global, ignores anthropological complexity and the planetary context. Yet it is not sufficient merely to brandish the flag of globality: One must associate the global elements within a complex, organizational articulation, and one must contextualize this very globality. The necessary reform in thinking is that which will generate a complex thinking in context.

It must be in planetary terms that we think about politics, the economy, demographics, ecology, and the protection of biological, ecological, and regional-cultural treasures, as in Amazonia, for instance, with both its indigenous cultures and its forests. Similarly, with regard to the protection of all animal, vegetable, and cultural diversities, the fruit of a multimillenial experiment is inseparable from ecological diversities, but it is not enough to insert all things and events within a planetary "framework" or "horizon." It is a question, rather, of always seeking out the relation of inseparability and of inter-retro-action between each phenomenon and its context and of every context with the planetary context.

THINKING THE COMPLEX

We need a kind of thinking that relinks that which is disjointed and compartmentalized, that respects diversity as it recognizes unity, and that tries to discern interdependencies. We need a radical thinking (which gets to the root of problems), a multidimensional thinking, and an organizational or systemic thinking, capable of conceiving the following recursive relation that has started to develop in the Earth sciences and the sciences of ecology:

We need an ecologized thinking that, instead of isolating the object being studied, considers it in and through its auto-eco-organizational relation to its cultural, social, economic, political, and natural environment. We need a thinking that grasps the principles of the ecology of action and the dialectics of action (see *Arguments*, 1990) and that would be capable of a strategy that allows for the modification, and even the nullification, of the action undertaken.

We need a thinking that recognizes its incompleteness and can deal with uncertainty, the unforeseen, interdependencies, and inter-retro-actions that quickly expand to a planetary scale, discontinuity, nonlinearity, disequilibrium, "chaotic" behavior, and bifurcations.

We must grasp not only the complexities of such inter-retro-actions, but also their hologrammatic character, which means not only that the part—the individual, the nation—is included in the whole—the planet—but also the whole in the part, as we previously discussed (see Chapter 1).

The particular becomes abstract as soon as it is isolated from its context, from the whole of which it is a part. The global becomes abstract as soon as it is detached from its parts. Thinking the planetary complex involves a ceaseless movement from the part to the whole and from the whole to the part. Pascal (1670/1931) can be taken at his word when he said: "Thus, all things being both caused and causing, assisted and assisting, mediated and immediate, and everything holding together through a natural and invisible bond that links the most distant and different, I hold it to be impossible to know the parts without knowing the whole, or to know the whole without a particular knowledge of the parts" (p. 91).

The complex formula of anthropolitics is not limited to the injunction, "think globally, act locally," but is rather expressed in the coupling of *think globally/act locally* with *think locally/act globally*. Planetary thinking ceases opposing the universal and the concrete, the general and the singular: The universal has become singular—it is the cosmic universe—it is the terrestrial universe.

To many, the loss of an abstract universalism seems like the loss of the universal, and the loss of a pseudorationalism appears to the rationalizers like a rise of irrationalism.

Abstract and progressivist universalism is indeed in crisis, but in the very process wherein everything becomes global, and where everything is situated in this, our singular universe, the concrete universal is finally at hand.

THE RESTORATION OF THINKING

The disciplinary universe no longer leaves any room for thinking (see Morin, 1985). Philosophers and scientists obviously think, as do nonscientists and nonphilosophers, but thinking itself seems to be an ancillary activity of science and philosophy, whereas the latter are, by their very nature, dedicated to thinking about humanity, life, the world, and reality, and this thinking ought to retroact on consciousness/conscience and serve to orient living.

Clearly, the reform in thinking would require a reform in teaching (primary, secondary, university), which itself would require the reform in thinking. Just as clearly, the democratization of the right to thinking would require a paradigmatic revolution that would allow for a complex thinking to reorganize knowledge and relink the fragmented disciplines. Once again, we are faced with the inseparability of problems, with their circular or recursive character, in which each depends on the other. This makes the reform in thinking all the more difficult, and at the same time, all the more necessary, as only a complex thinking could consider and deal with this interdependent circularity.

The reform in thinking is a key anthropological and historical problem. This implies a mental revolution of considerably greater proportions than the Copernican revolution. Never before in the history of humanity have the responsibilities of thinking weighed so crushingly on us. Thinking about tragedy has itself become tragic.

8

The Gospel of Doom

LOST SALVATION, UNKNOWN ADVENTURE

Hypothetical space travelers, journeying through the galaxies of the Virgo cluster, would ignore the very marginal Milky Way and would move far away from the peripheral small sun, which holds within its orbit the tiny planet Earth. Like Robinson Crusoe on his island, we have sent signals to the stars, although thus far in vain, and perhaps eternally so. We are lost in the cosmos.

This awesome cosmos is itself doomed. Having been born, it is mortal. It expands at a maddening speed, as stars collide, explode, and implode. Our Sun, the successor to two or three other defunct suns, will itself burn out. All living beings are thrown into life without being asked and are destined for death without having wished it. They live between nothingness and nothingness, the one behind us, the other ahead, all the while surrounded by nothingness. It is not only individuals who are doomed, but, sooner or later, humankind, then the last traces of life, and finally the Earth. The cosmos itself is running to its death, whether through scattering itself in all directions or through returning implosively to its origin. From this dead cosmos perhaps another will rise, but our cosmos will then be irremediably dead. Our cosmos is doomed. We are lost.

This cosmos of ours has a very weak foundation and is almost insubstantial: It came into existence by accident, perhaps from a fission of the infinite, unless one wants to say that it sprang from nothingness. Be that as it may, known matter makes up only a very small part of this small part. To our minds, it is the organizations made of material components, such as atoms, molecules, stars, and living beings, that stand out as substantive and real. It is the qualities arising from these organizations, such as life, consciousness, beauty, and love, that for us are valuable. However, these qualities are evanescent and transient, like the blooming flower, a shining face, love's labor lost.

Life, consciousness, love, truth, and beauty are short-lived. These marvelous qualities build on organizations of organizations, on unbelievable luck, and they constantly run deadly risks. For us, they are basic, but they themselves have no basis. There is no absolute basis to anything anyway, as everything stems in the last or first analysis from namelessness and formlessness. Everything is born in contingency, and whatever is born is destined to death.

Nevertheless, the ultimate qualities, the ultimate products of evolution, such as consciousness and love, must be acknowledged as the first norms and the first laws.

These qualities will not attain perfection or immutability. Love and consciousness will die. Nothing will escape death. There is no salvation in the sense of religions that promise personal immortality. There is no earthly salvation, as promised by the communist religion, that is a social solution, in which the life of all and everyone would be freed from misfortune, uncertainty, and tragedy. We must forsake this salvation radically and definitively.

We must also renounce infinite expectations. Western humanism is devoted to the conquest of nature without limit. The law of progress told us that progress had to be pursued endlessly. There was to be no limit to economic growth, to human intelligence, to reason. Humankind had become for itself its own infinite. We can today dismiss these false infinites and become aware of our irremediable finiteness. In the words of Gadamer, we must "stop conceptualizing finiteness as the limit which our infinite will-to-be cannot cross, and understand finiteness in positive terms, as the true fundamental law of *Dasein*." The genuine infinite lies beyond human reason, intellect, and powers. Perhaps it permeates us through and through, totally invisible, foreshadowed only in poetry and music.

Together with the awareness of finiteness, we can henceforth acquire an awareness of our unawareness and a knowledge of our ignorance: We can know from now on that we are in an unknown adventure. Believing in pseudoscience, we have thought that we knew the meaning of human history. However, from the dawn of humankind and from the dawn of historical times, we were already launched on an unknown adventure, and we continue to be now more than ever. The course followed by the Planetary Era has wrenched it free from the reiterative time of traditional civilizations and opened for it a future always more uncertain.

We are fated to the uncertainty that the religions of salvation, including the faith in earthly salvation, believed to have overcome: "The bolcheviks did not want, or could not understand that man is a weak and dubious being, doing something dubious in a dubious world" (Tchossitch, 1990, p.186).

It should not escape us that existence in a physical world (and the physical world itself) has paid an unbelievable price in damage, loss and ruin; that living existence has paid an unbelievable price in sufferings; that every human joy or happiness has been and will continue to be paid for by damage, loss, ruin, and sufferings.

We are wandering. We do not tread a well-marked path. We can no longer use the law of progress as a radar. We have no messiah, no salvation. We are ambling along through night and fog. We do not wander at random, even though there is randomness in our stride, because we can also have a beacon—ideas, chosen values, and strategy—that gets better as it goes along. It is not as if we are walking to the slaughterhouse. We are driven by our longings and are endowed with will and courage. Wandering feeds on hope, but a hope deprived of any ultimate reward and navigating on an ocean of despair.

Our wandering is this-worldly and bound to the fate of the Earth. Nonetheless, it also involves a quest for the beyond. Not a beyond outside of the world, but a beyond relative to the *hic et nunc*, to misery and misfortune, an unknown beyond that is proper to the unknown adventure.

Wandering is a context for real life. It enhances the authentic, poetic, and ecstatic moments of existence, and, on the other side, because any attained goal opens onto a new road and any solution raises a new problem, it disparages to some extent the ideas of goal and solution. Time can be fully experienced within wandering, not only as a continuum tying together past/present/future, but also as a regeneration (past), action (present), and possibility (future).

We are in an unknown adventure. Wandering is resumed because we are dissatisfied, but it will never satisfy. We must bear with doubt and anxiety. We must take *Dasein* seriously: the fact of "being there" without knowing why. There will be a growing number of reasons to be anxious, and a growing need for participation, fervor, and fellowship, which alone can suppress—not annihilate—anxiety. Love is the antidote, the counterthrust—not the answer—to anxiety.

Such is the fundamentally positive experience of the human being, in which communion and exaltation of self and other are brought to their utmost when they are not possessive. Could we not, as it were, thaw the huge amount of love petrified in religions and abstractions and devote it to the mortal, no longer to the immortal?

THE GOOD-BAD NEWS

Doom will remain enshrined in our destiny. Such is the bad news: We are lost, irretrievably lost. If there is a gospel, that is a good news, it must arise from the bad: Yes, we are lost, but we have a roof, a house, a country, namely, the small planet where life has created its garden, where humans have constructed their home, in which humankind must henceforth recognize its common abode.

It is not an Eden; it is our country, the place of our shared life and death destiny. We must till our earthly garden—that is, civilize the Earth.

The gospel of lost humankind and of Homeland Earth enjoins us to be *brothers/sisters*, not because we are saved, but because we are lost.[1] Let us be *brothers/sisters* in order to implement genuinely in life and death our common terrestrial fate. Let us be *brothers/sisters,* as we share the unknown adventure.

Albert Cohen (1972) has said: "That this dreadful adventure of humans arriving, laughing, moving, then suddenly not moving anymore, that this impending catastrophe leave us immune to kindness and pity, is indeed unbelievable."

The bad news is not new: From the first awakening of the human mind, there has been an awareness of doom: but this awareness has been dismissed by the belief in life after death, then by the hope of salvation. Nevertheless, everyone is attended in secret by the idea of doom; everyone carries it more or less deeply in themselves. The good news is not new either: The gospel of lost humans renews the message of compassion and commiseration of the Prince Sakyamuni and the sermon on the mount of Jesus of Nazareth, but at the core of the bad news, there is neither salvation through preservation/resurrection of the self, nor deliverance through its cosmic dispersion.

---

[1] As a matter of fact, the idea of salvation, or doom denied, subconsciously involved the idea of doom. Every religion of life beyond death carried and repressed the consciousness of death as irreparable.

THE CALL FOR FELLOWSHIP

The call for fellowship does not extend only to a race, a class, an elite, or a nation. It proceeds from those who, wherever they may be, hear it in themselves, and it is meant for all and everyone. Everywhere, in all classes, in all nations, are to be found people of "good will" for whom its message is their message. Perhaps there are more such people among the anxious, the curious, the open-minded, the kind, the halfbred, the bastards, and other betwixt and between.

The call for fellowship should not only overcome the stickiness and imperviousness of indifference, but also enmity. The existence of an enemy fosters both their barbarousness and my own. Even when resulting from a onesided blindness, enmity becomes reciprocal as soon as felt enmity makes us hostile in turn. Of course, ego- and ethnocentrisms, which have made and go on making enemies, are unfailing structures of individuality and subjectivity (Morin, 1985). However, the same way this structure entails a principle of exclusion in the *I*, so it also entails a principle of inclusion in the *we*. The key issue for leading humanity to its fulfillment is to widen the *we*, to encompass within the earthly matripatriotic relation any *ego alter*, and to acknowledge him or her as an *alter ego*, that is, a human brother or sister.

We must overcome our aversion to that which does not conform to our norms and taboos, our enmity for strangers, unto whom we project our fear of the unknown and of strangeness. The stranger should reciprocate, but someone must take the initiative.

Enemies sometimes kill, rape, and torture, but we cannot cut them out of the human species, and we cannot shut ourselves against the possibility of repentance. The complex idea of multipersonality teaches us that there are many persons within one individual, and that we cannot enclose this individual within his or her criminal person. To define human beings as criminal, said Hegel, is tantamount to disowning all their other human features that are not criminal. No one should be condemned forever. Magnanimity, repentance, and forgiveness show us how to stop the vicious circle of vendetta, punishment, and vengeance, that threatens both "us" and "them." We must jam the infernal machine that, always and everywhere, makes cruelty out of cruelty. Here again, we must not look for Edenic solutions to these problems, but fight against horrors because, as we have seen, one of the deeply set planetary goals is resistance to the cruelty of the world.[2]

---

[2] We also know that a great difficulty is to be able to live without a scapegoat. Scapegoating has deep animal roots in us, as well as typically human ones nourished by our torments, worries, and anxieties.

LIVING ON EARTH FOR LIFE'S SAKE

I would expand the line from Hoelderlin by saying: We dwell on Earth both prosaically and poetically. Prosaically (when we work, aim at practical targets, try to survive), and poetically (when we sing, dream, enjoy and love, admire).

Human life is prose and poetry woven together. Poetry is not only a literary genre, but also a way of life involving participation, love, eagerness, communion, enthusiasm, ritual, feast, intoxication, dance, and song, which in effect transfigures prosaic life made of practical, utilitarian, and technical chores. Furthermore, each and every human being speaks two languages with its mother tongue. The first denotes and objectivizes and is based on the law of the excluded middle. The second rather speaks through connotation, which is the halo of contextual significations surrounding every word or phrase, toys with analogy and metaphor, tries to translate emotions and sentiments, and allows the soul to manifest itself. Two states, often separate, are also present in us, the first or prosaic one answers to rational/empirical activities, and the state rightly called "second"—the poetic state—is brought about not only by poetry, but also by music, dance, festivity, jollity, and love and reaches its highest point in ecstasy. When in the poetic state, the second state is the first.

Fernando Pessoa used to say that there are two beings in each of us. The first, the true one, is the one of visions and dreams, born during childhood and lasting throughout life; the second, the false one, is the one made of externals, of words and actions. We can put it this way: Within us, two beings reside, the one prosaic, the other poetical. These two beings or states make up our being, they are its two mutually indispensable polarities. Prose in particular is a prerequisite of poetry, and the poetic state as such cannot appear except on the backdrop of the prosaic state.

The prosaic state sets up for us a utilitarian and functional situation with its goal being utilitarian and functional.

The poetic state can be linked to loving or brotherly/sisterly goals, but it is also an end in itself. The two states may oppose each other, exist side by side, or mix together. In archaic societies, they interacted closely; daily work, the grinding of flour, for instance, was accompanied by songs and marked with rhythm. The preparation for hunting or war involved mimetic rituals made of songs and dances. Traditional civilizations hinged on the alternation between festivities—when taboos were lifted and when enthusiasm, spending, intoxication, and destruction prevailed—and daily life, burdened with constraints and bound by frugality and parsimony.

Modern Western civilization has separated prose and poetry. It has made festivities scarce and to some extent drained them to the benefit of leisure, a catch-all notion that everyone fills as best they can. The life of work and economic activity have been invaded by prose (the logic of profitableness, etc.)[3]; poetry has been relegated to private life, to leisure and vacations, and it has evolved in its own way through love affairs, games, sports, movies, and of course literature and poetry proper.[4]

Today, at the turn of the millennium, hyperprose has made progress through the logic of artificial machines which has invaded all spheres of existence, through the hypertrophy of the technobureaucratic world, and the spread of clock time, both overloaded and strained, at the expense of the natural time of living beings. The betrayal and collapse of the poetic hope in a universal victory of fellowship has spread a large blanket of prose over the world. On the ruins of the poetical promise to change life, ethnic and religious regenerations endeavor to reclaim the poetics of communal participation, while the prose of econocratism and technocratism, which turns politics into management, is triumphant in the Western world, no doubt only for a time, but for now at any rate. Now, granted that politics need not take upon itself the dream of doing away with world prose through the realization of earthly happiness, it does not follow that it should shut itself up in prose. This amounts to saying that the politics of humanity does not have as its sole target advanced industrial society, postindustrial society, or technical progress. The politics of development, in the sense discussed previously as inclusive of the idea of metadevelopment (see Chapter 4), involves the full awareness of humanity's poetical needs.

Such being the case, the spread of hyperprose calls for a powerful counteroffensive of poetry, which must go hand in hand with the revival of fellowship and the gospel of doom. As a matter of fact, awareness of Homeland Earth can by itself put us in a poetic state. The relation to Earth is esthetic, better still, loving, and

---

[3]There are, of course, poetic delights enjoyed by capitalists, managers, and so on, and that are based on the will-to-wealth and profit, on the exercise of leadership in enterprise, and stock market speculations.

[4]Literary poetry has revolted twice against prosaic, utilitarian, and bourgeois life: first, in the early 19th century, with romanticism, especially its original German variety, and second, in surrealism, which, like romanticism but more explicitly, signified poetry's protest against being reduced to literary expression pure and simple, and most of all its will to be incorporated in life. Surrealism wanted to continue Arthur Rimbaud's (1957) attempt at deprosifying daily life in order to unveil the wonders that lie hidden in the dirtiest or lowliest aspects of everyday existence.

sometimes ecstatic. How not to sway in ecstasy when, all of a sudden, a huge moon flashes unexpectedly on the horizon of the night? How not almost to swoon at the sight of flying swallows? Are they only marvelous flying machines; do they cry uniquely in order to convey some information? Are they not delighted and maddeningly thrilled by their swift turns and dives, their climbing skyward, brushing past yet never touching each other?

To reiterate, it is useless to envisage a permanent poetic state, which, in any case, if uninterrupted would become dull or else wild. We would be reviving, in a different way, the illusions of this-worldly salvation. We must abide by complementarity and the alternation of poetry and prose.

We have a vital need for prose because practical, prosaic activities help us survive. Already in the animal kingdom, survival activities (to look for food or for prey, to defend oneself against dangers or against aggressors) often fill the whole of life and preclude enjoyment. Today, on Earth, humans spend most of their life surviving.

We must strive to make the second state be the first. We must try to live for the sake of living and not only for sheer survival. Poetic life is precisely that: life for life's sake.

THE GOSPEL OF DOOM

What complexity is to thought, the gospel of fellowship is to ethics: it does not call for fragmentation and separation, but for links, and thus it is intrinsically religious, in the literal sense of the word (*re-legere*).

Religious—The word both embarrasses and puzzles. It is tied to too many divine contents, seemingly consubstantial with them, even though we mean it minimally—to relink (to tie again).

As a matter of fact, religion in the ordinary sense of the word is defined in terms opposite to those of the gospel of doom: a belief in gods or God, with worship and rituals. The religion of salvation promises a glorious life after death.

However, the religion of god(s) belongs to a first type of religion. Modern Europe has witnessed the appearance of godless religions that were unaware of being such and that we may call religions of the second type. Thus, the nation-state has exuded its own religion, followed by the lay, rational, and scientific sphere. Robespierre wanted a religion of reason; Auguste Comte thought he was founding a religion of humanity. Marx created a religion of this-worldly salvation, of self-styled scientific knowledge. It is even conceivable that the republican ethos of France's Third Republic had something religious about it, considering that it tied its faithful together by republican belief and civic ethics. Malraux prophesied that the 21st century will be religious because he had not seen that the 20th has been fanatically religious, although unaware of the religious nature of its ideologies.

The word *religion,* then, cannot be limited to god(s). Why then bother with the word *religion,* if we discard any religion of the second type (providence, salvation)? Because we need, in order to continue hominization and to civilize the Earth, *the power of communication and communion.*

In that sense, a religious impetus is required for the minds of people to be *relinked* together, and consequently for the will to be kindled, whereby problems will be linked one to the other.

Can we imagine an earthly religion of the third type—a religion of doom? If the gospel of lost humanity and of Homeland Earth could give rise to a religion, this religion would contrast sharply with religions of other-worldly salvation as much as with religions of this-worldly salvation, with belief in god(s) as well as with ideologies ignorant of their religious nature. However, such a religion would be able to encompass the other religions and help them retrace their origin. The antisalvation gospel can cooperate with the salvation gospel precisely on the basis of the ideal of fellowship they have in common.

Many of us already enact this religion as if in advance, although isolatedly, without as yet feeling the full force of communication and communion.

Such a religion would involve a rational undertaking: to save the planet, to civilize the Earth, to unify humankind while safeguarding its diversity. It would insure, not prohibit, the full employment of rational thinking and would take upon itself the lay, questioning, and self-critical thought stemming from the European Renaissance.

This would be a religion in the minimal sense, although not reducible to what is rational. There is indeed something sur-rational about it: to take part in what surpasses us, to let in what Pascal called charity and what we may call compassion. It includes a mystical and sacred sentiment. Perhaps it calls for a ritual, as every community needs communion. In rituals, wherein the faithful communicate, people experience a forceful identity tied to something *surrational* and *surreal,* which they call god(s).

Such a religion would be a godless religion, in which the absence of god would reveal an omnipresent mystery. Such a religion would be without revelation (like Buddhism), a religion of love (like

Christianity), of commiseration (like Buddhism), although without salvation of the immortal/risen self or deliverance through the dissipation of self.

Such a religion would be a depth religion, uniting people in suffering and death. It would not proffer any primary or ultimate truth. We do not know why the world is the world, why we exist, why we pass away; we do not know who we are. Such a religion would lack any providence, any shining hereafter, but would bind us together as fellows in the unknown adventure.

Such a religion would not have promises but roots: roots in our cultures and civilizations, in planetary and human history; roots in life; roots in the stars that have forged the atoms of which we are made; roots in the cosmos where the particles were born and out of which our atoms were made.

Such a religion would be terrestrial, not other-worldly, not even this-worldly or earthly if some kind of salvation is implied. It would not be a question of salvation, then, but of safeguard, rescue, liberation, and fellowship.

Such a religion would involve a belief, like all religions, but, unlike other religions that repress doubt through excessive zeal, it would make room for doubt within itself. It would cope with uncertainty. It would look out on the abyss.

Recognition of Homeland Earth, then, meets with the religion of lost mortals, or rather flows into this religion of doom. There is no salvation if the word means to escape doom. However, if salvation means to dodge the worst, to find out what is best, then our personal salvation lies in consciousness, love, and fellowship. Our collective salvation has to do with preventing the disaster of a premature death for humankind and making of the Earth, lost in the cosmos, a "heaven haven."

Conclusion:
Homeland Earth

Now that the fantastic adventure begun in the 15th century has come to an end, the shout of Columbus' lookout man takes on at last a planetary meaning: Land! Land![1]

Even up to 1950-1960, we were living on a misapprehended Earth, on an abstract Earth. We were living on the Earth as object. By the end of this century, we discovered Earth as system, as Gaia, as biosphere, a cosmic speck—Homeland Earth. Each one of us has a pedigree, a terrestrial identity card. We are from, in, and on the Earth. We belong to the Earth which belongs to us.

THE GREAT CONFLUENCE

At this turn of the millennium, we have reached almost simultaneously a point at which many complementary forms of awareness have become possible:

- The awareness that Earth is one (telluric consciousness)

---

[1] In French, the same word: terre/Terre means both land and Earth.

- The awareness that the biosphere is unified/diversified (ecological consciousness)
- The awareness that humankind is one/many (anthropological consciousness)
- The awareness of our Dasein, of "being there," without knowing why
- The awareness of the Planetary Era
- The awareness of the Damoclean threat
- The awareness of the doom that looms at the horizon of our lives, of all life, of every planet, of every sun
- The awareness of our terrestrial fate.

Thanks to these modes of awareness, messages coming from the most diverse directions can henceforth converge; some of them religious, others ethical, humanist, romantic, or scientific, and others still relating to the Planetary Iron Age.

In this way, the humanist conception of the Enlightenment, that everyone has the same essence, can merge with a romantic feeling for nature, a feeling that rediscovered the umbilical relation to Mother Earth. At the same time, we can join our love of those both near and far—a love that has its distant origin in the great universalist religions, whether as Buddhist commiseration for all living beings, or as evangelical brotherliness, of which internationalist brotherliness has been but a lay socialist heir—to the emerging planetary consciousness, which links humans together and all to our common terrestrial nature.

All these messages have been obscured and have deteriorated over time, sometimes even turning into the opposite, through interaction with various institutions. They stand in need of unceasing regeneration, and perhaps they can regenerate each other through the gospel of doom. They are as so many disjointed fragments of a puzzle which, once completed, reveals the form of an anthropo-ethic.

HOMELAND EARTH

Mastery over nature? We are unable as yet to control our own nature, whose madness impels us to mastery over nature while losing our own self-control.

Master the world? We are as microbes in the gigantic and enigmatic cosmos. Mastery over life? Even if one day we could make a bacterium, we would have only copied an organism that forever leaves us dumbfounded. Would we know how to make a swallow, a buffalo, a sea lion, or an orchid? We can massacre billions of bacteria, but we cannot prevent resistant bacteria from propagating. We can kill viruses, but we are defenseless in front of new viruses that taunt us, undergo mutations and renewals. Even as far as bacteria and viruses are concerned, we are compelled to strike a deal with life and nature.

We have transformed the Earth, domesticated its vegetal surfaces, and gained mastery over its animals. We are not for all that masters of the cosmos, not even of the Earth.

To be gypsies of the cosmos, vagabonds of the unknown adventure, such is the anthropological destiny that comes to light from the depths of the fifth century of the Planetary Era, a destiny that follows on a multimillenial limitation to the repetitive cycle of traditional civilizations, to beliefs in eternity and supernatural myths. Such is our *Dasein*, to be, as it were, thrown on this Earth, wandering, treading untrodden paths, worried, anxious, but also full of dash, poetry, ecstasies. Such is *Homo sapiens demens*, an unbelievable "chimera," a new invention, a monster, a chaos, a subject of contradictions, of wonder—judge of all things, trustee of the truth and cesspool of doubt and errors; the "glory and rubbish of the universe," in the words of Pascal (1670/1931, p. 184), and such is *homo*, as already seen by Heraclitus, Eschylus, Sophocles, Shakespeare and, undoubtedly, many others in other cultures.

We must relearn our terrestrial finiteness and renounce the false infinite of technical omnipotence, of mental omnipotence, of our own yearning for omnipotence, so that we may bow to the true infinite that is unnamable and unconceivable. Our technical powers, thought, and consciousness must henceforth be devoted to fitting up, improving, and understanding, not to mastering.

We must learn to "be there" (*dasein*), on the planet—to be, to live, to share, to communicate and commune with one another. Self-enclosed cultures always knew and taught that wisdom. From now on, we must learn to be, to live, to share, to communicate and commune as human beings of planet Earth. We must transcend, without excluding, our local cultural identities, and awaken to our being as citizens of the Earth.

A COMMON EARTHLY FATE

Our homeland a planet? Such is our place in the cosmos.

We know now that this small, lost planet is more than a place jointly owned by humans. It is our home, *maison, Heimat*; it is our motherland, our Homeland. Neither suns nor space would provide us with a home: We would burn in the one place and turn into ice in the other. We might indeed someday leave the planet, whether to explore or to settle other worlds. These torrid or ice-cold worlds, however, are lifeless. It is here, at home, that are to be found our plants, our animals, our dead, our lives, and our children. We must preserve, we must save our Homeland.

Our "common earthly fate," then, proves to be singularly deep, vast, and timely. We all share a common destiny. We all live in the common garden of living beings and dwell in the common house of human beings. We are all drawn into the common adventure of the Planetary Era, all threatened by nuclear and ecological death. We are all subject to the struggles attending the turn of the millennium.

We must base human fellowship on the realization that we are lost, not on the illusion of salvation, but on the awareness of our participation in the complex web of the Planetary Era, on the awareness of our common death and life predicament, on the perception of the struggles attending this turn of the millennium.

The realization of our common earthly fate ought to be the key to this turn of the millennium: We are answerable for this planet; our life is bound to its life. We must put our household affairs in order.

We are citizens of the Earth and, thus, we share the same fate as the Earth.

CO-PILOTS OF THE EARTH

This shared destiny imposes a telluric responsibility on humankind. We must henceforth forsake the conquering agenda spelled out by Descartes, Buffon, and Marx. We must no longer strive to master the Earth, but to nurse it through its sickness, and learn how properly to dwell on it, to manage and cultivate it.

We humans must work toward a partnership with the terrestrial biosphere. To be sure, this will involve an unceasingly strenuous effort. In the process, we should not seek to pilot, but to co-pilot the Earth. A partnership is required: a partnership of humanity and nature, of technology and ecology, of conscious and unconscious intelligence. The Earth commands through life, humankind through consciousness.

To come through the Planetary Iron Age, to save humankind, to be co-pilots of the biosphere, to civilize the Earth—these four concepts are linked in a recursive loop, with each being necessary to the three others. The deadly sickness of the planet could then possibly mean rebirth—the emergence of a new humanity. Politics could be grounded anew. The old struggle for the survival of humankind would be absorbed into the struggle for the birth of humanity.

EARLY STAGES

The times are, to say the least, very harsh. Looking at the past, nothing is certain. The present is breaking apart. The future has collapsed. How is it possible not to doubt? The events of 1989-1990, which we took for a splendid sunrise, were nothing after all but the dazzling sight of an exploding supernova. But was it really an accident? Evolutionary processes, when speeded up, become explosions. As if moonstruck, the world is driven to a debacle as yet unseen. Homeland Earth, already so close, is still beyond reach. Disasters follow on disasters.

Civilize the Earth? Go from humankind to humanity? What can we expect of *Homo sapiens demens*? How can we ignore the gigantic and terrifying problem of human deficiencies? Always and everywhere, domination and exploitation have prevailed over mutual assistance and fellowship. Always and everywhere, hatred and contempt have prevailed over friendship and understanding. Until now, religions of love and ideologies of brotherhood have brought more hatred and disagreement than love and fellowship.

Throughout history, madness and unconsciousness have more often than not swept away reason and consciousness. Why should folly and unconsciousness, one more time, not settle our destiny?

Today, indeed, how blind seem traditionalists, modernists, and postmodernists. How fragmented is people's thinking. How unrecognized is planetary complexity. Such general unconsciousness of key issues. Such barbarousness in human relations. Such slackness of spirit and soul. There are so many misunderstandings.

Progress in the wake of culture? Not so long ago nazism made barbarous the most cultured country of the world. Saint-Germain-des-Prés or the Sorbonne providing a standard for humankind? Would that quell meanness, envy, or wickedness? Would that procure clear-headedness and the knowledge of our situation in the world?

Progress in the wake of civilization? Civilization is only a thin crust, cracked and defective, bringing about as many new problems as it solves. Freud's diagnosis of the disease of civilization (that civilizations have become neurotic owing to the civilizations themselves) applies also and especially to our own. When excessively civilized, a civilization fosters a craving for barbarism, as John Boorman has shown in *Zardoz*.

What does it mean, then, to civilize the Earth, if culture and civilization themselves are part of the problem? It means—and we are thus brought back to our main argument—that culture and civilization do not procure salvation. Nonetheless, through the very discontent brought on by its contentment, civilization feeds anthropological discontent all over again, and with it the pursuit of hominization. The discontent of contentment that has arisen in our civilization, and that undermines it, is precisely what may pave the way for its further evolution.

Once again, we meet with the principle of resistance. Finally, we have at our disposal the principles of hope within hopelessness. The first has to do with life itself: As every living being regenerates itself through being non-coercively directed toward its future, so do all human beings renew their hope while regenerating their life. Not that hope builds up life, because it is rather life that builds hope, but the best formula is the following: life builds up hope that builds up life.

The second principle has to do with foreknowledge: All the great transformations or creations have been unthinkable until they actually came to pass.

The third principle has to do with probability: All the happy events of history have always been a priori improbable.

The fourth principle is that of the mole that digs underground and transforms the substratum before anything is changed on the surface.

The fifth principle has to do with the possibility of rescue through the awareness of danger. In the words of Höelderlin (1980): ". . . where danger threatens/That which saves from it also grows" (p. 463).

The sixth principle is anthropological: We know that *Homo sapiens* has thus far made use only of a very small portion of its mind/brain potential, so that we are far from having exhausted the intellectual, emotional, cultural, civilizational, social, and political capabilities of humankind. The point is that our current culture is on a par with the still-present prehistory of the human mind, and that our current civilization is on a par with the still-present Planetary Iron Age. What this especially means is that, barring a possible catastrophe, we have not reached the limit of human brain/mind potential, of societies' historical possibilities, or of human evolution's anthropological capability. We may well be disillusioned and envisage nonetheless a new stage of hominization, which would also be a new stage of culture and civilization.

These six principles apply equally in the worst-case scenario. They give no assurance. Life may accidentally meet with death. The unthinkable will not necessarily come to pass. The improbable is not necessarily felicitous. The mole may destroy what ought to have been preserved. Rescue may be unequal to the peril.

The adventure remains unknown. The Planetary Era may possibly come to naught before it has even begun to bloom. Perhaps humankind's struggles may lead only to death and ruin. However, the worst is not yet certain, and the game is not yet over. In the absence of any certainty or even probability, there is the possibility of a better world.

The task is huge and unassured. We cannot eschew either hope or despair. Both holding of and resignation from office seem equally impossible. We must have a "passionate patience." We stand on the threshold, not of the last, but of the early stages of the battle.

References

Allégre, C. (1992). *Introduction à une histoire naturelle* [Introduction to a natural history]. Paris: Fayard.

Bastien, C. (1992, October). Le décalage entre logique et connaissance [The gap between logic and knowledge]. *Sciences Cognitives, 79.*

Benjamin, W. (1970). *Illuminations* (H. Arendt, ed., H. Zahn, trans.). London: Jonathan Cape.

Bronowski, J. (1969). *Concepts in the evolution of complexity.* Boston: American Association for the Advancement of Science.

Cohen, A. (1972). *O vous, frères humains* [Oh you, human brothers]. Paris: Gallimard.

Colloque de Cerisy. (1990). *Arguments pour une méthode* [Arguments for a method]. Paris: Editions du Seuil.

Crick, F. (1968). *Of molecules and men.* Seattle: University of Washington Press.

Danchin, A. (1990). *Une aurore de pierre* [Stone dawn]. Paris: Editions du Seuil.

Eibl-Eibesfeldt, I. (1971). *Love and hate.* New York: Holt Rinehart and Winston.

Eibl-Eibesfeldt, I. (1972). Similarities and differences between cultures in expressive movements. In R. Hinde (Ed.), *Non verbal communication* (pp. 297ff). Cambridge: Cambridge University Press.

Eibl-Eibesfeldt, I. (1974). Les universaux de comportement et leur genese [The universals of behavior and their genesis]. In M. Piatelli-Palmarini (Ed.), *L'unité de l'homme* [The unity of humankind] (pp. 233ff). Paris: Editions du Seuil.

Eigen, M. (1972). Self-organisation of the matter and the evolution of biological molecules. *Naturwissenschaft, 58,* 465.

Ferris, T. (1988). *Coming of age in the Milky Way.* New York: Morrow.

Freud, S. (1930). *Civilization and its discontents.* New York: Norton Library.

Gideon, S. (1948). *Mechanization takes command.* Oxford: Oxford University Press.

Hamburger, M. (Trans.). (1980). *Friederich Hölderlin.* Cambridge: Cambridge University Press.

Hoelderlin, F. (1980). *Patmos* (M. Hamburger, trans.). Cambridge: Cambridge University Press.

Korber, S. (1990). *Foreign Policy, 79,* 3-24.

Krell, D.F. (Trans.). (1985, Fall). The oldest program towards a system in German idealism. *The Owl of Minerva, 17*(1), 10.

Maruyama, M. (1992). Dysfunctional, misfunctional and toxifunctional aspects of cultures. *Technological Forecasting and Social Change, 42,* 301-307.

McLuhan, M. 1989. *The global village.* New York: Oxford University Press.

Morin, E. (1969). *Introduction à une politique de l'homme* [Introduction to a politics of humanity]. Paris: Editions du Seuil.

Morin, E. (1979). *Le paradigme perdu* [Paradigm lost]. Paris: Editions du Seuil.

Morin, E. (1981). *La méthode* [Method] *Vol. 1: La nature de la nature* [The nature of nature]. Paris: Editions du Seuil.

Morin, E. (1981). *Pour sortir du xxe siècle* [Surviving the 20th century]. Paris: Editions du Seuil.

Morin, E. (1983). *De la nature de l'U.R.S.S.* [On the nature of the Soviet Union]. Paris: Fayard.

Morin, E. (1985). *La méthode* [Method] *Vol. 2: La vie de la vie* [The life of life]. Paris: Editions du Seuil.

Morin, E. (1987). *Penser l'Europe* [The idea of Europe]. Paris: Gallimard.

Morin, E. (1990). *Introduction à la pensée complexe* [Introduction to complex thought]. Paris: ESF.

Morin, E. (1991). *La méthode* [Method] Vol 4: *Les idées* [Ideas]. Paris: Editions du Seuil.

Morin, E. (1992). *La méthode* [Method] *Vol. 3: La connaissance de la connaissance* [The knowing of knowing]. Paris: Editions du Seuil.

Morin, E. (1994). *Sociologie* [Sociology]. Paris: Fayard.

Morin, E., & Piattelli-Palmarini, M. (1974). *L'unité de l'homme* [The unity of humankind]. Paris: Stock.

Paillard, B. (1981). *La damnation de Fos* [The damnation of Fos]. Paris: Editions du Seuil.

Pascal, B. (1931). *Pensées* [Thoughts]. (L. Brunschwicg, ed.). Paris: Hachette. (Original work published 1670)

Passet, R. (1992, May). *Les Echos* [Echoes].

Prigogine, I. (1984). *Order out of chaos*. Toronto: Bantam Books.

Recanati, F. (1992, October). *La pragmatique linguistique* [Linguistic pragmatics]. *Sciences Cognitives, 79*, 21.

Rimbaud, A. (1957). *Illuminations* (L. Varèse, trans.). New York: New Directions.

Ritzer, G. (1992). *The Macdonaldization of society*. Newbury Park, CA: Sage.

Tchossitch, D. (1990). *Le temps de mal* [The period of evil]. Paris: L'Age d'Homme.

Van Lawick-Goodall, J. (1971). *The shadow of man*. London: Collins.

von Foerster, H., & Zopf, G.W. (1962). *Principles of self-organization*. New York: Pergamon.

von Neumann, J. (1966). *Theory of self-reproducing automata*. Urbana: University of Illinois Press.

CPSIA information can be obtained at www.ICGtesting.com
Printed in the USA
LVOW011357141111

254873LV00001B/5/P